WINNING
Court Testimony for
Law Enforcement Officers

The Law, Art & Science of
Effective Court Communication

MATTHEW J. MEDINA

43-08 162nd Street
Flushing, NY 11358
www.LooseleafLaw.com
800-647-5547

Library of Congress Cataloging-in-Publication
Medina, Matthew.
 Winning court testimony for law enforcement officers : the law, art & science of effective court communication / Matthew J. Medina.
  p. cm.
 Includes bibliographical references and index.
 ISBN 978-1-60885-036-5
 1. Police witnesses--United States--Handbooks, manuals, etc. I. Title.
 KF9672.M43 2012
 345.73'066--dc23
          2012019560

Cover by *Sans Serif,* Saline, Michigan

TABLE OF CONTENTS

DEDICATION

> **Dedicated To My Son,
> Matthew Joseph Medina II**
>
> Matty likes to throw rocks in rivers and
> splash in puddles.
>
> He wanted me to remind my readers
> that "freight trains are too loud!"
>
> Matty will be 4 years old next month.
>
> Matty, I love you more than anything in
> the whole wide world.

ACKNOWLEDGMENTS

I would like to thank Cook County Sheriff's Police Detective, Nick Ditusa, and Prospect Heights Police Commander, Al Steffen, for their extremely valuable contributions to this book. Nick is now retired from over twenty-seven years' service with Cook County. Detective Ditusa and his partners solved thousands of the most serious crimes. Because of Nick's exceptional skills, the latter part of his career he was assigned to the Cook County Sheriff's Department's elite Cold Case Homicide Unit. In the short time he spent with Cold Case before he retired, he and his partner managed to solve homicides dating as far back as 1978. He has testified for the prosecution in hundreds of bench and jury trials.

I point out Nick's background and experience because of all of his proud accomplishments. Nick took the time to write me a letter saying that one of his proudest moments occurred in a case where his side actually lost. As a prosecutor, I knew the case. In this case the judge stated in open court, "This detective has been in front of me for many years... when he testifies in front of me, I never question what he says because he [always] speaks the truth." Nick's lesson about the importance of developing a reputation for honesty appear throughout this book.

ABOUT THE AUTHOR

Matthew J. Medina received his Juris Doctor degree from the University of Illinois College of Law and has been a member of the Illinois Bar since 1996.

After thirteen years, Mr. Medina left the Cook County State's Attorneys Office so that he could expand his consulting, teaching and writing in the areas of criminal law and procedure.

Last count, Mr. Medina had appeared on behalf of the People of the State of Illinois 3,832 times. He prosecuted everything from traffic tickets to Class X felonies. He is now in private practice and is writing another law book tentatively entitled *Fog Everywhere: How To Use The Music Of Poetry And The Rhetoric Of Literature In Opening And Closing Statements.*

Mr. Medina loves to spend time with his son Matty and also loves to throw rocks in rivers.

PROLOGUE

"Big Mud" is twenty buildings made mostly of gray cement and reinforced steel. It occupies 78 acres of formerly fertile Illinois farm land. Now the land is the home of thorn-weed, poison oak and prisoners. Frank lives here now, in Big Muddy River Correctional Center. If you ask the Cook County State's Attorney, Frank chose his own fate when he decided to commit an armed robbery. If you ask Frank, he'll tell you he's incarcerated at Big Mud because of his incompetent lawyer. We may never know who is right. There is one thing we do know for sure, *not a single juror believed* Frank's star alibi witness.

Frank will be at Big Mud for the next six to thirty years if you want to talk with him about his case. As for me, I am puzzled. Why did the jury believe the testimony of witness B, the prosecution's witness and discount or disbelieve the testimony of witness A, the defense alibi witness? My attempt to answer this question is the heart of this book.

One day, not too long ago, I was chicken-pecking my keyboard trying to learn the new computer system in my office. Randomly, and quite by accident, I discovered a surprising fact. Well, surprising to *me* anyway. I have appeared in court on behalf of the People of the State of Illinois over three thousand times in my career. Before you conclude that I am 100 years old, most of these court appearances were *not* jury trials. My court appearances were much like that of the average attorney, mundane and ministerial. There are not many *"The truth?! You can't handle the truth!"* moments in real-life law practice. The following example is typical. **Me**: *"Judge, the State is asking for a continuance in order to re-subpoena a necessary witness."* **Judge**: *"What date are you seeking?"* **Me**: *"12th?"* **Judge**: *"That'll be the Order."* Wow! I got credit for *that*?

Having appeared over three thousand times in the Cook County Criminal Court system, I have had the privilege of watching a lot of court proceedings. What's the value in *watching*? Surely you learn more by *doing* than *watching*. Right? Sort of. I have conducted hundreds of bench trials (trials before only a judge) and a dozen or so jury trials. Because of these court cases, I've had the opportunity to conduct countless direct and cross-examinations of witnesses. I have learned a lot about what effective testimony looks like from behind the podium. Experience is a great teacher. This is true for two reasons. Experience permits practice. And (more importantly) experience gives you the opportunity to make mistakes. These two important teachers—practice and mistake making—are *only* learned by *doing*.

I have had the great opportunity to make many mistakes in real time. A *non-fatal*[1] mistake, the type inexperienced attorneys make every day in court, is the factory that forges either greater understanding of the trial process or change of career.[2] I learned, for example, the rudimentary law that it is always a good idea to learn the names of your witnesses. One time I was conducting a preliminary hearing on a simple drug case. I called to the witness stand Officer Susan Jones. I should have known something was amiss when she gave me a befuddled look while swearing to tell the truth. After I asked her a few preliminary questions I got right to the point.

Me: "Officer Jones can you point to the person that you arrested in this case and identify what he or she is wearing—for purpose of court identification."

**Officer
Jones**:   "No."

That is when I realized that she was NOT the arresting officer. The arresting officer was *Samantha* Jones—right police department—wrong police officer. This was not one of my prouder moments as a prosecutor. *Learn the names of your witnesses!* OK. I think I'll remember that nugget of wisdom forever. Learn by doing. There is another equally and often overlooked learning tool: watching.

The value in watching court cases as an attentive outsider is simple. When you are a prosecutor trying the case, or a defense attorney defending his or her client, you miss a lot. Trial attorneys tend to become narrowly focused on the immediate task at hand. This is especially true during a jury trial. It is very easy to get wrapped up in the immediacy of the moment. The ability to narrowly focus on the most important task, which is the task you are doing *now*, is common to all successful trial attorneys.

There is nothing wrong with focused concentration. However, every act of attention involves a trade-off. Focusing on *this* means ignoring *that*. That is precisely what it means to focus. If your goal is to ask this witness a precise question, a question not subject to ambiguity or misinterpretation, then you better ignore everything else. There will be plenty of time to wonder if you left your car lights on. There will be plenty of time to perform a mental check-list of what you need to pick up from the grocery store on the way home from court. *A loaf of bread, a gallon of milk, and a stick of butter...*

Where was I? Oh. Focus involves compromise. Often, when focused, you miss the many instructive subtleties that take place in every court case. For example:

> *Juror #3 yawned after you asked your last question. The witness grimaced when you looked down at your notes. Juror #5 (the juror you thought was going to be "the leader" in jury deliberations) keeps falling asleep. The judge is not paying attention. The guy in the front row of the public gallery is giving the defendant the "stink-eye." Juror #6 noticed that the guy in the front row of the public gallery is giving the defendant the "stink-eye."* And so on.

The same witness, sitting in the same witness chair, answering the same questions, can appear different to different people. How a witness is perceived depends largely on who is doing the perceiving. What is your perspective? Are you the attorney asking the questions? Are you watching court because it's raining outside and the courtroom is a nice warm place to sit while you wait for the storm to pass? Are you a juror? There are as many motivations for being in the courtroom watching a witness testify as there are people watching in the courtroom.

I have always been motivated by the desire to figure out what makes a witness believable. Why did the jury believe *this* witness and not *that* witness? This question has always been in the back of my mind in every case I have ever watched or tried. I am lucky to have had the privilege to watch some of the best trial attorneys in the country prepare witnesses to testify in criminal court. I have had the opportunity to see what worked and what didn't. I have seen firsthand that the best witness, that is, the *effective witness*, is not a type of witness; he or she is not a type of person; the effective witness is more a result than a person. The best results come from excellent collaboration between the attorney who asks the questions and the witness who answers them. All the other skills can be learned.

I used the word *effective* when I defined the *best witnesses*. What is an effective witness? Later in this book I will provide a more complete definition of what I mean by effective. For now, an effective witness is a witness who is understood and believed. That's it. Simple. Well, sort of.

Aristotle @ 26ᵗʰ & California

My inquiry into what makes an effective witness has taken me from Athens, Greece (2700 years ago) to the present day. I had a plan when I began to research this book First, I would read thousands upon thousands of pages of court transcripts. Second, I would read every recent cutting-edge study I could get my hands on. Third, I sat in courtrooms at 26 Street & California Avenue, the Cook County Illinois Criminal Courts Building, and watched lots and lots of court cases. Fourth, I lurked in the back of courtrooms from the suburban districts of Cook County to the rural and farmland counties of Kane and Boon in Illinois. I wanted to get a flavor of how things worked that went beyond my own experience of trying cases. I wanted to learn from attorneys vastly better than me. Fifth, I researched in the fields of communications, jury dynamics, psychology, social psychology, and behavioral economics. My goal was to provide my readers with the most up to date information possible. Finally, as an afterthought, I read a few of the classics in the field of rhetoric. My intention here was to provide an historical perspective on this topic.

Something unexpected happened to me after I read Aristotle's *Rhetoric*—for *historical* perspective. It hit me like an anvil dropped on my head from an overpass: many of Aristotle's intuitions about what makes a person believable, what makes a speaker persuasive, intuitions that he had 2700 years ago, have been confirmed by contemporary studies. It turns out that Aristotle was right all along.

This discovery caused me to expand my research. Instead of reading the likes of Aristotle, Cicero and Shakespeare (to give just three examples) for just historical perspective, I decided to see which, if any, of their intuitions regarding effective communication have been confirmed[3] by the contemporary literature. Do not misunderstand. Not all experts agree with each other. Not all scientific studies are "scientific." Some of the studies I read were tightly controlled and their conclusions were well reasoned. Other

studies were just an ink-blot short of psychobabble. The courtroom is not a controlled laboratory and testifying is not an exact
science. Even so, common themes began to emerge when I started
to compare what I learned in the literature with what I observed
in the courtroom. I found that there are principles of effective
court communication that are historically, scientifically, prac-
tically, and intuitively accurate.

The above research leads to the following methodology. Every
principle in this book had to meet each of four criteria. First, each
idea had to have deep historical precedents.[4] Second, each
principle needed to be corroborated in contemporary studies and
law reviews. Third, each principle must work in the real world. If
I didn't see the principle work in the live courtroom,[5] I did not
include the principle in this book. Fourth, the principle had to
make intuitive or common sense. What follows are the principles
that made the cut.

People (witnesses) want to be believed, and people (jurors) do
not want to be deceived. Deception is a part of almost every living
community from the ant to the aardvark. Even plants deceive.
The issue of deception is present in almost all great literature.
However, deception is rarely *about* deception; but rather, its
detection (or its lack of *timely* detection). How do we know we are
being lied to? I'll give you the short answer—skip this part if you
desire not to spoil show—we don't. Lie detectors are great
investigative tools. Lie detectors encourage defendants to confess.
They are often successful because many defendants *think* they
work. Apologies to my Chicago Police and FBI friends, but you
might as well toss chicken bones on the floor and use their
configuration to divine whether a person is lying. The chicken
bone technique couldn't be less accurate than a lie detector test.
But ever since humankind invented the chicken-bone technique
of lie detection, we have been searching for reliable lie detectors.

The reason that so much of the wisdom and so many of the
studies regarding truth detection are contradictory is because
human nature is contradictory. We are natural lie detectors. But
we are not very good at detecting lies.[6] We are also natural liars.
But most of us are not very good at lying. Where does that leave
us? To be or not to be believed; that really is the question.

> *My very words, and despite their pride*
> *and passion they believed me. So by day*
> *I'd weave at my great and growing*
> *web—by night ... I would unravel all I'd*
> *done.*[7]
>   — **Homer** (from *The Odyssey*)

This book is for people who have never testified before as well as experienced prosecution witnesses. If you are a first-time witness you will learn what to expect on the witness stand. You will learn the best way to calm your nerves and testify effectively. You will learn basic principles of effective oral communication that apply in the special context of court testimony. On the other hand, if you are experienced and the courtroom fits you like an old pair of jeans prepare to learn that some of the basic wisdom that you have learned over the years (*–speak slowly–*) might be wrong.[8] Experienced witnesses will also be gratified to know that some of their basic common sense notions about how to speak in court are very likely correct (*–speak loudly–*).

INTRODUCTION

The courtroom was quiet. Surprisingly few people watched the proceedings. It was April 19, 2005, and the wooden benches, which not by accident look like church pews,[9] were almost empty. Other than some vague muffled voices coming from the hallway, everything was silent and still. The afternoon sun shone through cracks in the closed blinds; through the beams of light you could see flakes of paint chips falling off the ceiling like tiny faint gray snowflakes. Everything was still and quiet.

Assistant Cook County State's Attorney (ASA) Steven Rosenblum stood silently. He faced the jury. He stood alone in the middle of the courtroom about four feet in front of the jury box. Before ASA Rosenblum spoke he made eye contact with each juror one at a time.

ASA Rosenblum started to speak. He started slowly. Although his voice was soft, it carried a low tone that made it resonate to the back of the courtroom where I was sitting:

> Long Grove is a small suburban town located in the heart of Lake County, truly a beautiful setting where the land is open and nature is abundant. It's a long way from the main city of Chicago out to Long Grove, and because of its distance from that location, the population base is smaller out there. For the most part, it's [apart] from the big hustle and bustle of the big city, and it's replaced by the serenity of mother earth.

[Imperceptibly, while ASA Rosenblum was describing the scene of serenity and Mother Earth, he was moving slowly toward the defense table. He stopped and stood behind the defendant. If you weren't watching, you would not have noticed he was moving while speaking. The defendant was not sure where to look. The defendant turned to look at ASA Rosenblum. The defendant twisted around, uncomfortable; Mr. Rosenblum loomed behind him.]
[ASA Rosenblum paused.]
[The clock ticked –one-two-three-four-five-six-seven.]
[Now standing directly behind the defendant.]

ASA Rosenblum continued:

> *But there is a place out there that does exist. It's down in Long Grove, through the thigh-high prairie grass that encompasses the land, through the prickly branches of the towering pines that reach out of the earth. It's beyond the wire fence that separates the prairie from the dense forest. In that thick brush, just an inch below the surface of the mud floor, a young girl was encased in her grave." Nothing marked [the little girl's] grave, not a headstone, not a cross or marker of any sort; [she] was left dumped in a shallow grave in Long Grove, bruised, beaten, assaulted, strangled, and suffocated. Her body showed the trauma that she had endured. This is Skyler Chambers. He was much more streetwise than [this little girl] when he lured her into his car, that fourteen-year-old innocent child ...*[10]

That is how the prosecution began in the *People of the State of Illinois v. Skyler Chambers*. ASA Rosenblum made no overt argument.[11] He did not use a single word of legal jargon. He did not even tell the story in chronological order. ASA Rosenblum chose to begin his statement of facts in the middle of the story. He talked about what the scene looked like after the defendant committed the murder. There will be plenty of time for the members of the jury to consider the thousands of small details of the police investigation. First words are important. Arguably, the first words spoken to the jury are the *most* important. [See Chapter 1, Prosecution's Case-In Chief.] The prosecutor chose to use this opportunity to demonstrate through the use of vivid imagery the purpose and importance of their shared attention.

Before ASA Rosenblum said "This is Skyler Chambers," he needed to accomplish one modest goal. This jury would possibly have to sit through mind-numbing technical details (DNA) and boring, tedious details (hair fiber expert), etc. ASA Rosenblum used his introduction to the jury as an opportunity to share with them, in the clearest of terms, their shared solemn purpose.

Don't forget why we are here.

He wants every juror to think to his- or herself:

An innocent little girl lay in a shallow grave. She didn't get there by herself. She didn't have to be there. It didn't have to end this way. But it did. Not by luck or chance or fate. It was someone's purpose to murder her and dump her in that shallow grave. Somebody's choice; that somebody is here today sitting in this courtroom. And that is why I am here.

I was in the courtroom and listened to this opening statement. The prosecutor rarely raised his voice. He was calm, even-tempered, and under control. Even when he stepped over by the defendant's table, pointed and said, "This is Skyler Chambers ..." I could only detect a *slight* change in tone—from sadness/melancholy to disgust/indignation. He did not overdo it. He was just stating facts. His voice cracked slightly when he said the words "shallow grave." Even the most seasoned prosecutors, the ones most detached and professional, cannot and hide their humanity. This was no exception.

Now let us hear a different account of the *same crime*. This opening statement, unlike the one above, is fictional. This time I am going to replace the language chosen by Mr. Rosenblum with typical lawyer language. The language of the following opening statement is unfortunately all too typical in criminal courtrooms. See which argument you prefer.

Ladies and gentlemen of this honorable jury, I want to thank you for invaluable service to our court system and our Democratic Republic ... (5 more minutes of speaking about of why jury service is important and the jury's valuable role in our free society.) *Now then: this is a case about an innocent girl cruelly and callously murdered by the Defendant. Let there be no doubt, ladies and gentlemen of this Honorable Jury, the evidence will invariably show malicious aforethought. The State will prove beyond a reasonable doubt that the defendant acted with the specific intent to commit a homicide when, in a manner befitting a hardened criminal, he raped and killed this little girl. The evidence will also show that in an attempt to conceal his wanton acts of violence, the defendant committed another crime; the crime of concealment of a homicidal murder ...*

Most people prefer the first opening statement over the second. Why? Both statements of fact attempt to highlight the theme of "stolen innocence." Both statements set the table for the specific evidence the prosecution intends to show at trial. Both statements highlight the serious nature of the offense. Why is the first statement better than the second?

Look at the words.

Mr. Rosenblum used simple, everyday words. He chose the type of words that you can touch and feel. You know what "prairie grass" looks like, smells like, feels like. Everyone can imagine a "small town." What could be more beautiful and fresh than "towering pines"? These words represent *things*, real things. Things you can touch, prairie grass, land, prickly branches, brush. Who doesn't fear the "shallow grave"? The "luring" of a child is every parent's nightmare.

Now let us consider the words used in the second statement of facts. What does "malicious aforethought" look like? What does it mean for one to "act with specific intent"? Could the phrase "in a manner befitting a hardened criminal," be any vaguer? Why does the typical lawyer spend the first five minutes of his statement of facts giving the jury a civics lesson? That is the judge's job. Why the false flattery?

Words Matter

Opening Statement One

- small town
- beautiful
- land
- mother earth
- nature
- hustle and bustle
- towering pines
- prairie grass
- forest
- brush
- young girl
- child

Contrast

- encased
- grave
- suffocated
- headstone
- strangled
- left
- dumped

- shallow grave
- bruised
- beaten
- assaulted
- trauma
- lured

Opening Statement Two

- honorable
- invaluable
- system
- service
- democratic republic

- let there be no doubt
- valuable role
- Honorable Jury
- free society

Contrast

- cruelly
- callously
- specific intent
- prove
- reasonable doubt
- befitting
- commit homicide

- aforethought
- killed
- homicidal murder
- wanton
- evidence
- raped

What does this have to do with testifying on behalf of the state?

Almost everything you need to know about effective testimony is embedded in the above example. Principles like "use simple direct words"; "Tell a story"; "Tell the truth"; "Don't talk down to people"; "Speak like a person not a robot"; "Be yourself"; "Prepare"; and more are contained in the first opening statement. The second opening statement shows where things can go wrong.

The principles in this book can be used by civilian witnesses, police officers, detectives, investigators, private detectives, evidence technicians, forensic investigators medical examiners, security guards, loss prevention officers, federal agents, doctors, nurses, paramedics, fire fighters, arson investigators, lawyers, paralegals, and law students. You can apply the principles that you will learn in this book to almost any situation where you are called on to speak in a formal setting.

My goal is to teach you how to testify effectively. What do I mean by the word "effectively"? Effective testimony has four characteristics: it is **TR**uthful, **U**nderstandable, **T**rustworthy and **H**oned. An easy way to remember the four characteristics of effective testimony is to remember to always tell the *truth*.

Truthful

Aristotle, Greek philosopher and personal tutor to Alexander the Great, recognized in the fourth century B.C.E. that it was "impossible to separate the *credibility of the speaker* [from the] *credibility of the message.*"[12] Aristotle taught that gaining a reputation for truth telling is one of the most important steps to becoming a persuasive speaker. This is fortunate because if you are going to testify on behalf of the prosecution you need to understand that you are not just an ordinary witness. You adopt a special greater responsibility to *tell the truth, the whole truth, and nothing but the truth*. The prosecution has a special responsibility to the public.[13] A prosecutor's duty is to seek justice.[14] As the prosecution's witness, you should adopt the same high standard. If you are still reading this book I assume that you do. Your duty to tell the truth and your ability to be persuasive are linked.[15]

Understandable

An effective witness is very easy to understand. Understanding is not simply a function of using the right words. Understanding comes from bridging the gap between *you* and *them*. To bridge this gap there must be a tight fit between the words you use and the message you are trying to communicate. That is, *say what you mean.*[16] There also should be a tight fit between the message you are trying to communicate and the audience to whom your message is intended. That is, your audience needs to be receptive. Making yourself understood is always challenging when you are communicating with strangers. This task is made more difficult in a court of law because of two additional factors. First, in court you can't simply say what you want in any way you want to say it. Your speech is limited by rules of evidence. Second, witnesses in a court of law are only permitted to answer questions posed by someone else. And this third party, whether he or she is the prosecutor or the defense attorney, is constrained by the rules of evidence and the unique customs of criminal court. That is, you cannot simply say what you want; you can only answer questions. And the person asking you questions cannot simply ask whatever question he or she wants to; he or she must follow certain rules.

At first you might find it more difficult to get your point across in court than in another setting; but this book will teach you simple techniques to use to ensure that the jury understands your message. You will learn to use simple words and use them with precision. You will learn to say what you need to say and nothing more. You will learn to avoid using jargon. You will learn to provide accurate and descriptive details. You will learn how the proper use of volume and voice tone contributes to better understanding.

Trustworthy

You need to tell the truth if you want to be trustworthy. However, telling the truth is not enough. If you want to be worthy of the jury's trust then you must learn to how to *appear* trustworthy. You can tell the truth until the cows come home; if the jury does not believe you it doesn't matter. Your demeanor, the way you look, dress, act, and speak, in large part determines whether or not people believe you. Do you exhibit good eye contact? Who are you supposed to be looking at anyway, the judge, the jury, the questioner? Do you appear nervous?[17] Do you exhibit any unusual tics? Do you tap your feet when you are uncomfortable?[18] Do you ramble on and on and on? Do you have a natural smile? Do you know what you are talking about? Do these things matter? Yes.

Honed

> *Master the stuff, and the words will*
> *freely follow.*[19]
> — **Horace**

A honed witness is relaxed, polished, and completely in control. If you want to be a honed witness, you need to know your stuff and practice what you know. The more you learn about the court process in general, and your specific role in that process, the better honed you will be. If you have never testified in court, there is nothing more assuring than knowing what to expect and what is expected of you. Even if you have testified in court on many previous occasions, you may not be completely aware of the court process, which is understandable. Often witnesses, especially law enforcement witnesses, simply re-read their report, testify, and then go home. There is nothing wrong with this for the average witness. However, you don't want to be an average witness. You want to be honed.

The prosecutor told you that she may need you to testify on rebuttal. What does that mean? Perhaps you received a subpoena to testify in the prosecution's case-in-chief. How is that different from testifying in rebuttal? What exactly should you be doing before your court date? How should you dress for court? If, for example, you didn't even see the gunman's face, what is the prosecution attempting to achieve with your testimony? What paperwork should you review? What is the defense attorney likely to ask you? Why? The honed witness understands where his testimony fits in the scheme of the prosecution generally. The honed witness also knows where his or her testimony fits into the specific case.

Three Things to Keep in Mind

First

Anybody can learn how to testify effectively. Testifying in a criminal case, or any case for that matter, is not natural. What I mean by "not natural" is that it is not one of those "either-you-have-it-or-you-don't" skills. You can learn how to testify. It is a skill that can be taught. Simply acknowledging this fact can make you more confident, which, in turn, will make you more effective when you take the witness stand.

Second

When you learn the context of your testimony you become a better witness. This book is crammed with specific techniques you can use to make your testimony better. However, these techniques work best when you are clear about where your testimony fits in the theme of the prosecution's case. You need to know not only the basic structure of a criminal trial, but also the specific purpose of your testimony. This is why this book includes the study of effective argument as well as examples of what types of defenses the defendant is likely to use at trial. Witnesses do not argue anything. This is true; however, the better you understand what each side is doing the better your testimony will be.

Third

The best way to improve your skills is to practice them. This book will give you the confidence to receive every subpoena as a welcome opportunity to practice your new skills.

> *Indeed, good verbal communication, especially when describing past events, often is the ability to create for the decision-maker a mental image of what is being communicated.*[20]
>
> — **Fred Galves**
> (From *Harvard Journal Law and Technology*)

SECTION I

THE BASICS

> *Let the language devoted to truth be plain and simple.* [21]
>   — **Seneca**

OUTLINE

Section Overview

Trials are extremely unpredictable. Nobody knows exactly what questions the defense attorney will ask or what evidence the judge might permit or exclude. The only thing that a witness or attorney can control is the level of preparation. The more prepared you are the better your testimony will be. As you continue through this book you will learn that preparation does not mean that you should testify from a script or memorize your testimony. As paradoxical as it sounds, the best prepared witnesses are perceived as more spontaneous, natural, and truthful rather than less. The natural enemy of all public speaking is anxiety. The best way for you to reduce anxiety is to be prepared.

We will learn in the later chapters of this section the practical side of this subject. How do you prepare for court? You will learn exactly what it is you are expected to do before your court date arrives. You will also learn the strategic benefits of truth telling. The best tool of persuasion a person has is his or her reputation for truth telling. Finally, this section will teach you what exactly it means to be a prosecution witness. You will learn how this differs from being a defense witness. You will discover that courtroom demeanor counts and that a witness will always benefit from learning the courtroom rules of the road.

CHAPTER ONE
Anatomy of a Jury Trial

A defendant has the right to be tried by a jury of his peers.[22] If the defendant wishes, he can waive that right and have a trial before a judge called a bench trial. In this book, unless otherwise noted, I will assume that you are a witness who will be testifying before a jury. The guidelines presented in this book apply to both jury and bench trials unless noted otherwise. The basic structure of a jury trial, with some minor variations, is fairly uniform from state to state.

OPENING STATEMENTS

After jury selection is complete, each side, if they wish, may make an opening statement to the jury. The prosecution goes first followed by the defense. Opening statements are like movie trailers. They are reviews of coming attractions. Each side is permitted to tell the jury what they expect the facts will be at trial. Opening statements are not arguments. Attorneys are not permitted to make arguments in opening statements. Attorneys are permitted to argue during closing arguments and rebuttal argument at the end of each side's case.

PROSECUTION'S CASE-IN-CHIEF

Prosecution has the burden of proof so the prosecution gets to go first.[23] After the prosecution completes his opening statement, he will call his first witness. That might be you. Prosecutors have different theories concerning witness order. (*Strongest witness first—strongest witness last—bury bad witness in the middle* of trial, preferably a time right *before lunch* when the jury is not paying attention—etc.) You should not pay too much attention to what order you are testifying in relation to the other witnesses. First, prosecutors do not agree among themselves about what constitutes the "best" order to call witnesses. Second, even if they did, the dynamics of a jury trial are extremely fluid—plans change—so you may not testify in the order the prosecutor originally intended.

There are some common rules of thumb that many prosecutors use in deciding witness order. Generally, a prosecutor will call his best witness first and his second best witness last (or reverse). The reason for this is to take advantage of the natural psychological biases people have when they make decisions. The well-studied psychological biases known as the "primacy effect" (first thing heard) and "recency effect" (last thing heard) show that people are more likely to remember the *first* and *last* things they hear. They tend to forget what they heard in the muddled middle.[24]

Whenever you do testify, however, the order of questioning is likely to be the same. The prosecution will ask you questions. The prosecutor will ask you open-ended questions. This part is called the direct examination. Open-ended questions are questions that do not suggest the answer. Every case is different. However, in all cases the prosecution will ask you to share with the jury some of your basic information. The members of the jury are going to want to know the answer to the following two questions:

"Who are you?" and *"Why are you here?"*

The answer to these questions is always the same. I am a witness (who is a person like you with a name and identity that is apart from my role here) and I have something important to share with you. You accomplish this by answering a few short and relatively non-intrusive biographical questions. After you introduce yourself the prosecutor will usually jump right into the "Why you are here" part. The prosecutor will direct your attention to the date time and location of the incident and, where appropriate, ask you to identify the defendant.

Typical First Questions
Non-Law Enforcement

1. Please introduce yourself to the jury. (*My name is Forrest, Forrest Gump"*)

2. Would you kindly spell your name for the court reporter?

3. What do you do for a living? (*I'm a shrimping boat captain.*)

4. How long have you been a shrimping boat captain?

5. I'd like to ask you about events that took place on _____, 2012.

6. Do you recall what happened on that date?

7. Do you see in court today the person that ... (*Robbed you; you saw running from the bank,* etc.)

8. Can you point to that person and identify what he or she is wearing? (Actually point. Do not just say "The guy sitting next to the defense attorney.")

Typical First Questions
Law Enforcement

1. Please introduce yourself to the jury. (*My name is ...,* badge #, Department, Unit of Assignment.")

2. Would you kindly spell your name for the court reporter?

3. How long have you been a Chicago Police Detective?

4. Before you were promoted to detective how long were you employed by the Chicago Police Department as a sworn officer?

5. To become a sworn officer, what, if any, specialized training, tests or exams did you have to complete successfully? Explain.

6. Since your graduation from the police academy, have you had any further training or continuing education? Explain.

7. Before you were accepted into the Chicago Police Department what did you do for a living?

8. What do Chicago Police Detectives do? What are your specific duties as a detective?

9. Did you become involved in an investigation of (crime) on or about _____, 2012?

10. How did you become involved in this investigation?

When the prosecutor is finished the defense attorney will have an opportunity to cross-examine you. The difference between cross and direct is that the cross-examiner can ask you leading questions. A leading question is a question that suggests its own answer. (See Sections II & III.) After the defense is finished asking you questions on cross-examination the prosecutor is permitted to conduct a re-direct examination. Most good prosecutors will decline to ask you questions on re-direct. Re-direct is sort of a tacit admission that the defense cross-examination hurt. Theoretically, the cycle of direct-cross-re-direct-re-cross can go on forever.

PROSECUTION RESTS

After the prosecutor puts on all of his witnesses and evidence he will rest his case. The defense will present (usually oral) motion for the judge to toss the case based on their contention that evidence the prosecution's evidence is insufficient to support a finding of guilty beyond a reasonable doubt. This motion is not actually called motion to toss. Jurisdictions call this motion by different names: "Motion for Directed Verdict," "Motion to Dismiss," "Motion for Directed Finding," and other names. They are all the same. When the judge considers this motion she looks at the evidence in the light most favorable to the prosecution. Judges rarely grant these motions even if the prosecution's case is weak. Judges do not like to take the case out of the hands of the jury unless the prosecution's case is really, really bad.

DEFENSE CASE-IN-CHIEF

The defense can, but is not required to, call witnesses. The defendant can simply rest on his or her contention that the prosecution did not meet the burden of proof.[25] The defendant does not have to prove anything. The defendant may choose to testify or not. The decision whether or not to testify is the defendant's alone. Nobody can force the defendant to testify if he wishes not to. Nobody can prevent the defendant from testifying if he wishes to take the witness stand in his own defense. If the defendant chooses to call witnesses or testify himself or both, the order of questioning will proceed the same way it did in the prosecution's case-in-chief.

DEFENSE RESTS CASE-IN-CHIEF

The defense rests when he or she has no more evidence to present to the jury.

PROSECUTION'S REBUTTAL CASE

The prosecution can choose to call witnesses to rebut the defense witnesses. Or they can chose not to call witnesses in rebuttal. The only limitation is that the prosecution's rebuttal witnesses have to respond in some way to what the defense witnesses asserted. Rebuttal cannot be used as an "Oops! I forgot" opportunity to put on brand new evidence.

PROSECUTION RESTS IN REBUTTAL

Prosecution runs out of rebuttal witnesses.

DEFENSE SUR-REBUTTAL

Defense Sur-Rebuttal is its opportunity to rebut the prosecution's rebuttal case. You see where this is going, right? Theoretically, the cycle of rebuttal–Sur-Rebuttal can go on forever.

PROSECUTION'S OPENING-CLOSE

Prosecutors generally work with at least one partner when they try a case before a jury. One prosecutor will argue the Opening – Close and the other will argue in Rebuttal. The more experienced prosecutor generally argues Rebuttal and will assign the less experienced prosecutor the Opening – Close.[26] The closing argument that you see on TV or in the movies, the argument that usually forms the high point of every crime-court drama, is really a combination of the prosecution's Opening – Close and Rebuttal arguments. In fact, in its pure form, the prosecution's Rebuttal argument's content is closer to what people think of when they envision the typical "closing argument." Prosecution's Opening – Close boils down to this:

"This is the Law" (more here)

"This is how we proved the defendant guilty beyond a reasonable doubt." (More here)

"Please sign the guilty verdict form."

Opening – Close is less flashy than the prosecution's Rebuttal argument. The main reason for this is that the defense gets to respond to the prosecution's Opening – Close. Prosecutors like to keep their best zingers for the end—the defense has to sit and take it; unable to respond.

DEFENSE CLOSE

The defense's closing argument combines the elements of the prosecution's Opening-Close and the prosecution's rebuttal argument. The defense only gets one shot. Once the defense attorney is done with his argument he is done. The prosecution has the last word. The defense attorney will try to convince the jury to accept the defense theory of the case and at the same time anticipate and react to what the prosecution *might* say in rebuttal. This may be why the defense closing argument is usually longer than the prosecution's Opening-Close. The defense attorney has to both argue and rebut the prosecution's argument (part of which the defense has not yet heard).

PROSECUTION REBUTTAL ARGUMENT

This is the fun part.[27] The prosecutor has the opportunity to argue last. He receives the benefit of being the last person to influence the jury members before they deliberate. We learned that people tend to remember the first and last things they hear with greater ease than they remember things they hear in the muddled middle.[28] The best part, from the prosecutor's perspective, is that the defense cannot respond. Before concluding that giving the prosecutor the last word is unfair consider two facts. First, *somebody* has to speak last. Second, the prosecution has the burden of proof (as it should be). Prosecution's Rebuttal Argument boils down to this:

What? The Defense wants you to believe what?! (More here)

Let me give you 15 reasons why what he just said makes absolutely no sense. (More here)

Please sign the guilty verdict form.

POST-TRIAL MOTIONS

After the prosecution's rebuttal argument the judge will excuse the jury and the prosecution and defense will argue, on the record but outside the presence of the jury, various legal motions.[29]

JURY DELIBERATIONS

The jury will elect a foreperson from among its membership and begin their deliberations.

VERDICT

In all criminal cases the jury must reach a unanimous verdict. In most cases there are three possible outcomes. The jury will return a verdict of guilty. The jury will return a verdict of not guilty. The jury will return a mixed verdict guilty on some counts and not guilty on others. In rare cases the jury will be unable to reach a verdict on one or more of the charges. When a jury is unable to reach a unanimous decision on one or more charges it is called a "hung jury." Judges are reluctant to permit hung juries. When jurors cannot agree on a verdict, the foreperson will send a note to the judge to inform him or her that they are unable to reach a unanimous decision. The judge will almost always tell the jurors to keep deliberating. The judge will only declare a mistrial when the situation becomes hopeless. If the judge declares a mistrial the prosecution can re-try the defendant all over again.

POST-VERDICT MOTIONS

Once the jury reaches its verdict and that verdict is an-
nounced in open court the prosecution and defense will make
post-verdict motions to the court. If the jury finds the defendant
not guilty the matter is essentially over. There is not much the
prosecution can do about it—the jury has spoken. When the jury
returns a finding of guilty on one or more charge there are several
"typical" motions that the prosecution and defense will file with
the court. The defense usually will file "motion to dismiss
notwithstanding the jury's verdict."[30] This defense motion in
essence says to the judge that no reasonable jury could have
found the defendant guilty based on the evidence in this trial. It
is a request to the judge to overturn the jury verdict outright.
Judges rarely grant this motion even in cases where the judge
him- or herself would have found the defendant not guilty.
Traditionally, there must really be an extreme miscarriage of
justice before a judge will disturb a jury's verdict—even a verdict
he or she disagrees with. Another common motion is a prosecution motion. Usually, if the defendant has been "out on bond,"
that is, he has been free during trial because he posted a cash
bond, the prosecution will ask that the judge revoke the
defendant's bond and he be immediately taken into custody
pending appeal. Judges often grant this motion. The main reason
judges will revoke the defendant's bond after a verdict of guilty is
that once a jury finds the defendant guilty he is no longer
presumed innocent. He has been found guilty by a jury of his
peers and therefore will have to appeal his conviction from prison.

Review Chapter One

The Trial

- defendant has a constitutional right to a jury trial
- opening statement, prosecution goes first
- opening statements are not opening arguments
- each side is permitted to tell the jury what they expect the facts will be at trial
- prosecution's "case-in-chief" is a fancy way to say prosecution's main case
- prosecution has the burden of proof
- after opening statement the prosecution will call his first witness
- the first questions the prosecutor will ask will tell the jury who you are and why you are testifying
- the order of questions—direct-examination by prosecutor, then cross-examination by defense attorney, then re-direct by prosecutor, then re-cross by defense attorney
- prosecution rests case-in-chief when finished calling witnesses
- defense case-in-chief same as prosecution's
- defense does not have to call any witnesses
- the defense is not required to prove anything
- if defense calls witnesses prosecution may put on rebuttal witnesses
- defense can rebut the prosecution's rebuttal case this is called sur-rebuttal

The Arguments

- opening-close, prosecution goes first
- opening-close prosecution argues "this is the law and this is how we proved defendant guilty of violating this law"
- defense closing argument combines the prosecution's opening-close and the prosecution's rebuttal argument
- prosecution rebuttal argument prosecutor gets the last word
- post-trial motions
- jury deliberations
- verdict must be unanimous
- upon guilty verdict defense will ask the judge to find defendant not guilty anyway, the prosecution will ask that defendant's bond be revoked

Review Questions

True or False

1. Defendant cannot waive his right to be tried by jury.
2. The prosecution weakest witness generally testifies last.
3. Because of the "primacy effect," effective prosecutors will present their best arguments in their opening statement to the jury.
4. Except when asking questions of a preliminary nature, direct examination questions should open-ended.

Multiple Choice

1. If the jury finds the defendant not guilty of all charges the prosecutor may:
   a) quietly whimper to himself
   b) write a real crime novel called "Justice ... eh?"
   c) appeal only if the verdict is clearly a miscarriage of justice

   [ ]   (a) & (b)
   [ ]   all of the above
   [ ]   none of the above

2. After the prosecution rests its Case-in-Chief the defendant may:
   a) testify in his own defense
   b) call his own witnesses
   c) do absolutely nothing and stare at the wall

   [ ]   (a) & (b)
   [ ]   all of the above
   [ ]   none of the above

CHAPTER TWO
Prosecution Witness

> *... That we must become just by doing just acts, and temperate by doing temperate acts ...* [31]
>
> — **Aristotle**

Almost anybody can testify on behalf of the prosecution. In most respects, testifying for the prosecution is the same as testifying for the defense. A witness is qualified to testify if she is willing to swear or affirm to tell the truth and has personal knowledge of the matter about which she is testifying.[32] With few exceptions, almost everybody is qualified to testify in the courts of the United States. What makes testifying for the prosecution different is that the prosecution has the obligation to do justice. I know. YOU are not the prosecution. You are a witness. All that you have to do is tell the truth. True. However, the prosecutor has the right to expect that you will also respect the spirit of this obligation. You should expect this of yourself. What do I mean by the "spirit" of your obligation? The following joke by comedian Steven Wright illustrates my point:

> *I can't wait to be arrested and go all the way to the witness stand. 'Do you swear to tell the whole truth and nothing but the truth so help you, God?' Yes, you're ugly. See that woman in the jury? I'd really like to sleep with her. Should I keep going or are you going to ask me questions?* [33]
>
> — Steven Wright

There are ways to tell the truth and there are ways to tell the truth. Later in this book you will learn that you should answer only the question that the questioner asks you. Do not add anything to your answer that does not directly answer the question. Don't ramble, right? Right. Don't guess at what you think the questioner *meant* by his question. True. However, whenever the general guidelines of effective testimony conflict with your self-imposed higher standard of ethics (it rarely does), you should follow the higher standard of ethics. You should use your common sense notion of fairness. If the questioner (even the meanie defense attorney) asks a question that by its very nature shows that he has made an honest error, it is perfectly acceptable to be fair in your response.

> *I began my research on lying in every-day life with a bias—my belief that telling the whole truth is neither possible nor desirable, even if it were possible. Even the simplest of questions (e.g., "So, what did you do today?") can be answered in any number of ways, in any level of detail.* [34]
> — **Bella M. DePaulo**
> (From *The Many Faces of Lies*)

EXAMPLE

Q. *Isn't it true that on the night of 10-14-1066 you were at home all night?*
   A. [truthful answer] "No." Or "No, I wasn't born yet." Or "No, you are thinking of the Battle of Hastings—you know, the Norman Conquest of England!"
   B. [Fair answer] Yes, October 14, 2006, I was home all night.

Unless you watch court often, you might be surprised how many honest errors that attorneys and judges make. Of course the questioner meant 2006 and not 1066. The letter of the law your answer is no. The spirit of fairness the answer is yes—plus a very short rewording of the question. Be tough. But also be fair.

In a very real sense winning *isn't* everything. A prosecutor's obligation to seek justice means that he has a greater obligation than a defense attorney. The defense attorney's obligation is to advocate zealously in the interest of his or her client. Defense attorneys must perform their duties ethically. However, aside from following the rules of ethics, defense attorneys have no further obligations beyond advocating for his or her client. Prosecutors have the additional duty to seek justice because the prosecution is backed by the full weight of the government. The United States Supreme Court wrote eloquently about a prosecutor's special responsibility to seek justice in the case of *Berger v. United States*:

> *"The United States Attorney is the representative not of an ordinary party to a controversy, but of a sovereignty whose obligation to govern impartially is as compelling as its obligation to govern at all; and whose interest, therefore, in a criminal prosecution is not that it shall win a case, but that justice shall be done. As such, he is in a peculiar and very definite sense the servant of the law, the twofold aim of which is that guilt shall not escape or innocence suffer. He may prosecute with earnestness and vigor — indeed, he should do so. But, while he may strike hard blows, he is not at liberty to strike foul ones. It is as much his duty to refrain from improper methods calculated to produce a wrongful conviction as it is to use every legitimate means to bring about a just one."*[35]

State witnesses, like the prosecution itself, should hold themselves to a higher ethical standard. Why? Because it is the right thing to do. You should read everything in this book in light of your ethical obligation to do the right thing. If any technique or piece of advice in this book runs contrary to your ethical obligation to do the right thing in a particular circumstance, you must choose to do right over doing what wins.

The good news is that you can do both at the same time. In most cases, being ethical and truthful is *not* incompatible with winning. In fact, in later chapters you will learn that a person's reputation for honesty is his best weapon. The common sense notion that people tend to give greater weight to the testimony of a person whom they deem trustworthy goes back over 3000 years to Aristotle's Rhetoric and has been proven in contemporary studies. More on this later.

> *The primary safeguard against*
> *abuses ... is the ethical responsibility of*
> *the prosecutor, who, as so often has been*
> *said, may "strike hard blows" but not*
> *"foul ones."* [36]
> — ***United States v. Ash***

"In a criminal case the prosecution has the burden of establishing guilt solely on the basis of evidence produced in court and under circumstances assuring an accused all the safeguards of a fair procedure, among them the presumption of the defendant's innocence."[37] The court and the jury are required by law to presume the defendant's innocence. No such requirement exists for witnesses. In this book I encourage witnesses to conduct themselves in such a way as to go beyond the strict letter of the law. However, simply because a witness should hold herself up to the highest ethical standards does not mean she should abandon common sense. Witnesses, especially victims of crime, are not supposed to be unbiased. The very reason the prosecution called you to testify in the first place is because you have facts that the prosecution believes may be helpful in proving the defendant's guilt. This is not an unbiased position.

THE LAW ENFORCEMENT WITNESS

> *The prosecution has the duty to disclose*
> *evidence favorable to the defendant that*
> *is important to either his guilt or*
> *punishment.*[38]
> — ***Brady v. Maryland***

If you are a law enforcement officer you are held to a very high standard for truth telling for the reasons discussed above plus one. You have the unique powers granted to you by the state. The state gives you the authority to resolve disputes while they are happening. You can arrest and deprive people of their freedom. You have the power to use your common sense and impose your will on people. Society looks on you with respect and admiration. With great power comes great responsibility. People expect you to tell the truth. You likely hold yourself to a higher standard as well.

TRUTH TELLING AS TRIAL STRATEGY

Truth telling is an art form and not an on-off switch. There are ways to tell the truth effectively and ways to tell the truth ineffectively. The truth can be the most powerful tool in your rhetorical arsenal. Subject to your ethical obligations, which include the principle of fairness, the best approach to truth telling is the direct approach in most instances (submit to your self-imposed obligation to be fair).... One should tell the "naked truth." What is the "naked truth?" It is truth unembellished. It is truth without a spin or shade or caveat or explanation. The naked truth is simpler than "truth with explanation." When the question is "Was the light red?" the naked truth answer is "Yes," or "Yes, the light was red." (Or no). The "truth with explanation" answer to "Was the light red?" looks something like this: "Well—technically, but under the circumstances as it were.... blah, blah, blah ..."

How does this help your case when the truth is not on your side? The short answer: telling the truth *always* helps your case in the long run, and *usually* helps your case even in the short run. There are four reasons for this. The truth is usually simple. The truth is usually direct. The truth generally sounds like the truth. The truth makes sense in light of all the other facts known to the judge or jury. The best arguments are simple, direct, credible, and reasonable in light of all the evidence.

But even if the truth in your case is hard, complicated, unwieldy, and hard to believe, you must still tell the truth. It is the law. It is the right thing to do. But there are also specific rhetorical benefits to telling the truth. Many witnesses for the prosecution are repeat players. If you are a police officer, federal agent, loss prevention officer or really anybody who has to testify more than once in a criminal court setting it is to your advantage to develop a reputation for honesty. People will remember you. Judges and attorneys and court personnel talk to each other like any other group of people who work together—reputations, for better or worse—spread quickly, and follow you into every courtroom you set foot in. You cannot control the facts but, to a large extent, you do have control over your reputation.

Example #1

[The officer did not *see* defendant's light turn red. The officer assumed that the defendant's light was red because the officer's light was green. The officer was traveling north/south and defendant was traveling east/west.]

Q. Officer, isn't it true that you did not see the traffic light turn red when my client passed through the intersection?

A. No. My light was green, so no; your client's light was red. I was on facing north and your client was facing east. I know this intersection there is no delay ...

The answer to this question is "yes" or "That's true." Leave the answer stand without embellishments, commentary or snarkiness. Even if it seems appropriate to explain your answer, or provide a snarky answer to a snarky question, resist the urge. The prosecution will have the chance to clear up any misunderstanding about this question on his re-direct examination so relax. It is not your job to explain your answer.

If you want the jury to believe you, you must present yourself as a professional whose only desire is to provide objective facts. Embellishments, commentary, and snarkiness undermine this position. Even though you are not neutral, and you are testifying on behalf of one side over the other, that does not make you an advocate. Let the attorneys advocate. Let the prosecutor make the arguments.

In the following example the defense attorney is trying to make the point that the police officer did not have reasonable suspicion or probable cause to pull the defendant over. After it is established that this police officer pulled the defendant over the next questions are worded in such a way as to get the police officer to say "no." The officer does say no. The police officer did not take the bait. He told the truth. The police officer knows why he pulled the defendant over. The defense attorney also knows why the officer pulled the defendant over. The police officer had plenty of reasonable suspicion to pull over the defendant. The defendant (and the other person in the car) fit the description of two people who were suspects in a murder. Notice the defense attorney does

not ask about that. He asked specific questions that all merited a
"no" response from the police officer. The officer did the right thing
and answered "no" to each question. We will learn in the cross-
examination section of this book not to worry about the defense
attorney taking your words or actions out of context. The prosecution will have an opportunity to "rehabilitate" you. The prosecutor will have a chance to ask you questions and clear up any
confusion created by the defense attorney. Officer Miller did the
right thing. You can never go wrong when you stick to the truth.

Example #2 [39]

DEFENSE DIRECT EXAMINATION OF POLICE OFFICER[40]

Q. Did you take part in stopping that car?
A. Yes.
Q. Do you recall who was driving that car?
A. We were in two separate cars. Officer Miller was in the first
car and I was in the second car behind Officer Miller.

Q. Now prior to stopping that vehicle, did you see that vehicle
violate any traffic law?
A. No.
Q. At the time that you stopped that vehicle, did you have an
arrest warrant for Turner Reeves?
A. I didn't.
Q. Did you know if one existed?
A. I didn't know if one existed or not.
Q. At the time you stopped that vehicle, did you see Mr. Reeves
violate and State or Federal law in your presence?
A. No.
Q. From the time the vehicle was stopped from the time that Mr.
Reeves was taken from the scene by the police, how many
minutes elapsed?
A. I don't recall how many minutes?

STATE CROSS-EXAMINATION[41]

Q. At the time you were informed to make a stop on two
individuals, you knew the two individuals at the time you

were looking for were Turner Reeves and Skyler Chambers, [wanted for murder] is that correct?

A. Yes.

Q. In fact the descriptions that you had of those individuals [that you had] ... both individuals in that vehicle matched the descriptions that you had of Turner Reeves and Skyler Chambers, isn't that correct?

A. Yes.

Review Chapter Two

- nearly everybody is qualified to testify in the courts of the united states

- hold yourself to a higher ethical standard than what the law requires

- using common sense and treating people fairly are not prohibited court activities

- prosecution's goal must be that guilt shall not escape or innocence suffer

- in most instances tell the naked truth and avoid truth with explanation

- having a good reputation for honesty is your most valuable court asset

- when answering a question avoid embellishments, commentary and snarkiness

- let the prosecutor make the arguments, you just answer the questions

Review Questions

True or False

1. Almost anybody can testify in a court of law in the United States.
2. Witnesses must swear to tell the truth.
3. The prosecution has the obligation to seek justice even if that means dismissing the case.
4. But, while a prosecutor may strike hard blows, he is not at liberty to strike foul ones.
5. It is perfectly acceptable for you to treat opposing counsel with fairness.
6. You do not have to like the defense team or the defendant.

Fill in the Blank

1. You should read everything in this book in light of your ethical obligation to do the ____ ____. (Two words)
2. Ethical and truthful testimony is not incompatible with _____ testimony.
3. The prosecution has the duty to _____ evidence that is favorable to defendant.

Multiple Choice

1. Under your obligation to "tell the truth, the whole truth, and nothing but the truth," you must disclose to the court the following:

   a) if think the jury foreperson is cute
   b) that the judge smells nice
   c) that you almost never dress in a suit unless you are in a wedding or in court

   [ ] All of the above
   [ ] None of the above
   [ ] (a) and (b)
   [ ] (c)

T/F 1. T, 2. F, 3. T, 4. T, 5. T, 6. T

FITB 1. right thing, 2. winning or effective, 3. disclose

M/C 1. None of the above

CHAPTER THREE
What to Do Before Court

Find out well in advance of your court date whether you will meet the prosecutor in court or in his or her office. Often the court date on your subpoena or notice to appear is incorrect. This court date will sometimes be changed without you knowing about it. This happens more often than you might think. Often the defense or the prosecution will file a motion for continuance with the court. Court generally grants this type of motion. In case that one side asks for and is granted a continuance, the party asking for the continuance is supposed to notify the witnesses that the court date has changed. Sometimes people forget to do this.

Call the prosecutor a day or two in advance of the scheduled court date. Make sure that the court date hasn't changed. When you call the prosecutor's office make sure that you immediately identify yourself as a prosecution witness or victim. Prosecutors' offices receive countless calls from crackpots and bored people. In addition to crackpots and pranksters, some defendants will call the prosecutor's office seeking legal advice. So identify yourself. Tell the person answering the phone the name of the prosecutor assigned to your case. If you do not know the prosecutor assigned to your case, or one has yet to be assigned, have the case number handy. The case number should be somewhere in your subpoena or notice to appear. If you lost the notice then try to remember the name of the defendant. Having this information handy will lower (but not completely eliminate) the possibility that the person answering the phone will treat you like a crackpot.

Arrive early to court. Pretend that you are going to the airport if that helps. Dress how you would normally dress if you were going to a job interview. There are a couple of exceptions to this guideline. The prosecutor may instruct you to dress differently. Sometimes the prosecutor will forget to instruct you how to dress. It's OK to ask. There are countless strategic reasons a prosecutor might want you to dress a certain way. Listen to the prosecutor and follow her instructions. Trust the prosecutor. She has her reasons. If you are a law enforcement witness, your agency might require you wear your uniform while in court. —by all means wear what your boss tells you to wear—unless your boss tells you to wear something stupid or weird.

When the day comes when you must testify your testimony will begin much earlier than you might think. Your testimony will begin when you arrive in the parking lot or parking garage of the courthouse. It will continue as you wait in line at security. Your testimony will follow you into the halls of the courthouse and into the courtroom. There will be no break for lunch and you will not find reprieve on the escalator or in the elevator. Why? Because in any of these places you may encounter jurors. If you are obnoxious, loud or rude, the person standing next to you might very well become a member of the jury; the very jury that will hear your testimony; the jury that will be the sole judge of your credibility.

When you arrive to the courthouse you cannot know who might be selected to sit on the jury. You must therefore assume that any person that you encounter is a potential juror. So be polite and courteous to everybody.[42] Act as if you are already in the courtroom and facing the jury. You do not need to act as if you are at a solemn event like a funeral. Be yourself.[43] But simply be aware that the people around you are potential jurors. With the above in mind; try not to talk about your testimony in any public area, especially in confined areas such as elevators and narrow hallways. You never know who might be listening. If you need to discuss a matter involving your testimony and there are no private conference rooms available, make sure you do so quietly.

This advice is especially important after the parties have chosen the jury members. Very often judges will instruct a witness to remain in the courthouse after he or she has given testimony and been cross-examined by the defense. This is because one side or the other might want to call you back to the witness stand to give additional testimony.

There are several reasons why either side (or both sides) might call you to testify again. The most common reason for the prosecution or defense to call you again is to "rebut" the testimony of another person. If the judge, or either side, anticipates this might be the case, the judge will ask you to stay until you are released. Never leave the courthouse after you testify without getting the permission of the judge or prosecutor.

On some occasions both the prosecution and the defense instructed you to come to court. Generally the prosecution will either give you some sort of letter or verbal notice that you must be in court on a certain day and time. The defense usually will compel you to appear in court by serving you a court order called a subpoena or summons. If this is the case make sure that you tell the prosecutor before you leave court that you are under a defense subpoena. If the defense subpoenaed you then the prosecution must check with the defense as well as the judge before the judge will permit you to go home.

REASONS TO RELAX

> "'Give us your evidence,' said the King; 'and don't be nervous, or I'll have you executed on the spot.' This did not seem to encourage the witness at all..."
> — *Alice in Wonderland* [44]

Why Rules of Evidence are Like a Glass of Warm Milk and a Bedtime Story

In Chapter 4 of this book (Courtroom Demeanor) I explain how important it is for you to simply relax. Don't worry. Of course, this is easy for me to say (even easier to write), because I am not the person who is doing the testifying. True. However, there are some objective reasons not to worry about having to testify in an open public courtroom. Many of these reasons are written into the rules of evidence.[45] Often, the most frightening fear about testifying is the fear of "drawing a blank," "freezing-up," "spacing out,"—that is, you fear that while under the pressure of testifying, you might *forget everything* and simply sit there looking stupid until they have to drag you off the witness stand in a strait-jacket. I assure you that this will not happen.[46] If you forget, the prosecutor will simply refresh your memory.

EVIDENCE TIP

All courts permit the questioner to refresh a witness's memory if he or she forgets, freezes-up, blanks-out, or simply fails to remember a certain fact. So if you forget something just say so. The questioner will ask you if your memory is exhausted. If you say yes (You must *at least* remember to say yes!), then the questioner will ask you, "Will anything serve to refresh your memory?" Again—you say yes. Then simply tell the questioner whatever it is that will help you remember. Almost anything will do. The following are just a few examples of what most courts will permit the questioner to show you, if, by doing so, your memory will be refreshed:

- ✓ Your Notes
- ✓ Somebody Else's Notes
- ✓ The Police Report
- ✓ Somebody Else's Police Report
- ✓ Map
- ✓ Phone Book
- ✓ Pinecone
- ✓ Accident Report
- ✓ Medical Examiner's Report
- ✓ Any Cheese or Dairy Product
- ✓ My Book
- ✓ Anything

So, really, it's OK to relax. There are very few exceptions to the "you can have your memory refreshed by anything" rule. These exceptions are beyond the scope of this book and probably do not apply to your case anyway. A warning: Just because the prosecutor may refresh your memory does not mean that you should come to court unprepared. If you rely on this rule too often, the jury will likely conclude that your testimony is unreliable. Use—but use sparingly.

EVIDENCE TIP

Another Reason to Relax

We will look at cross-examination in depth in Section III of this book. Before you get yourself worked-up about being cross-examined, you should be aware that, like many other aspects of the trial process, being cross-examined is *not* like it appears on TV. Cross-examination can and often does become prickly—even heated; however, most judges will not let an attorney abuse a witness. Take Federal Rule of Evidence 611 (a) for example. This Rule puts in writing what most good judges do intuitively.

Federal Rule of Evidence 611 (a)

(a) **Control by court.** The court shall exercise reasonable control over the mode and order of interrogating witnesses and presenting evidence so as to (1) make the interrogation and presentation effective for the ascertainment of the truth, (2) avoid needless consumption of time, and (3) protect witnesses from harassment or undue embarrassment.[47]

Yet Another Reason to Relax

Try not to worry about the defense attorney twisting your words around or taking something you said or did out of context. The prosecution will have a chance to "rehabilitate" your testimony. "Rehabilitating" a witness is a fancy way of saying that "your" attorney will ask you questions on redirect examination (or in some cases cross-examination) in order to put your words or actions back into context. Relax. Don't worry. Tell the truth and the prosecutor will take care of the rest.

Review Chapter Three

- the court date on your subpoena or notice to appear is often incorrect

- call the prosecutor a day or two in advance of the scheduled court date

- when you call the prosecutor's office, identify yourself as a witness or victim immediately

- arrive early

- dress like you would dress for a job interview unless the prosecutor instructs you otherwise

- do not worry about drawing a blank, freezing-up or spacing-out

- prosecutor can and will refresh your memory if necessary

- the rules require the judge to protect witnesses from harassment or undue embarrassment

Review Questions

True or False

1. The prosecutor can refresh your memory with a pine cone.
2. The prosecutor can refresh your memory with a pine cone if a pine cone will refresh your memory.
3. Prepare if you want, but you are just wasting your time.
4. Relax.
5. If you rely on the prosecutor to refresh your memory too often, the jury will think you are an unreliable witness.
6. Any person who you encounter in and around the courthouse is a potential juror.

Multiple Choice

1. The judge's job, which is to exercise control over the courtroom, serves to advance the following interests:
   a) assists in the search for the truth
   b) saves time
   c) protects witnesses from harassment or undue embarrassment

   [ ]   All of the above
   [ ]   None of the above
   [ ]   (a) and (b)
   [ ]   (c)

T/F   1. F, 2. T, 3. F, 4. T, 5. T, 6. T
M/C   1. all of the above

CHAPTER FOUR
Persuasion

> *The best way to convince a skeptic that you are trustworthy ... is to be trustworthy.* [48]
>
> — **Steven Pinker**
> (From *The Blank Slate*)

One of your most important assets is your reputation. The best tool of persuasion a person has is his or her reputation for truth telling.[49] Telling the truth, even when it seems hurtful, wins cases. From the time Aristotle wrote his famous treatise *Rhetoric* in the fourth century B.C.E., to the present-day scholarship in behavioral economics, truth-telling has been recognized as an effective means of persuasion.[50]

> *Effective Communication*
>
> 1. *Trustworthy Speaker*
> 2. *Who Knows The Subject*
> 3. *Who Knows The Audience*[51]
>
> — **Aristotle**

Effective communication is truthful, clear, and persuasive.[52] If you find yourself having to testify on behalf of the prosecution there are concrete things that you can do to prepare yourself. Some of the rules of effective communication are common sense and some are not. Readers know (intuitively or otherwise) that if the jury likes you they are more likely to believe what you are saying than if they do not like you. This is common sense, right? Some common sense notions are true and some are not true. For example, readers know that you should always speak loudly and slowly so that everyone in the room can hear you and understand you. This truth is half right. You will learn that it's always good to speak *loudly* but not necessarily *slowly*.[53] Likeability does, however, have a great effect on believability.[54]

Courtrooms are forums of persuasion. As a witness for the prosecution, you presumably want the prosecution to win. There is nothing wrong or unethical about wanting your side to win. However, your job is not to persuade. Your job is to be understood, trusted, and believed. Your testimony should be truthful, factual, and objective, nothing more. Your testimony is not an argument. The prosecutor's job is to make arguments. It is the prosecutor's job to persuade the judge and jury.

> *Audience is affected by Credibility,*
> *Reason and Emotion.*[55]
>
>   — **Aristotle**

The best prosecution witnesses also understand that, although it is not the witnesses' job to make arguments, a good witness should know what the prosecution is trying to accomplish. Your testimony becomes one of the building blocks of the prosecutor's argument. If you testify well, the prosecution will use your testimony to build his case against the defendant; if you testify poorly the prosecution will be stuck with your testimony anyway. Prosecutors are bound by strict rules of ethical conduct. Most prosecutors also have an innate sense of duty not only to the rules specifically, but also to the idea of fairness in the courtroom. With this in mind, prosecutors also want to win. They win by persuading the judge and jury that their arguments are sound and their evidence strong. If it is not a witness's job to make arguments, or to persuade the judge and jury, then why learn about the art of persuasion? The most important practical reason for you to learn sound principles of persuasion is that it prepares you for what you are likely to encounter in the courtroom. I will repeat this theme throughout this book. The best witnesses are the most prepared witnesses.[56] If you want to be maximally prepared you need to understand more than simply your own testimony. You need to understand the trial process in general, and the specific role that your testimony will play in this process.

More than two thousand years after Aristotle's death in 322 B.C.E., he is still a major authority on the subject of persuasion.[57] His book *Rhetoric* is widely read in law and business schools. *Rhetoric* offers sound useful advice that is still relevant today. Aristotle advised people wishing to speak persuasively to master three topics. Two of these topics are appropriate in the criminal courtroom: ethos and logos. Aristotle's third rule for persuasive speaking, pathos (Emotion), is inappropriate in the special context of a criminal trial.[58]

Be Honest
(Aristotle's "Ethos")

First, effective persuasion begins with the speaker. Effective speakers have a reputation for honesty.

Know Your Stuff.
(Aristotle's "Logos")

Second, persuasive speakers have mastered their subject matter.

Effective Testimony =
(**T**ruthful/ **U**nderstandable/ **T**rustworthy & **H**oned)

We have learned much since the days of Aristotle. There have been incredible advances in the fields of human psychology, social psychology, behavioral economics, evolutionary psychology, and every field that touches on the nature and causes of human behavior. It turns out that Aristotle's intuitions were correct. People are more readily persuaded by likeable people who are versed in their subject matter and who know their audience well.[59]

Some findings are new. Some findings are surprising. People are not always as rational or calculating as once believed.[60] People sometimes make important decisions using mental short cuts rather than conscious rational deliberation.[61] All of these findings inform the art of persuasion.

How should you present yourself to a judge or jury? What is the best way to answer questions so that the judge and jury understand that you are telling the truth? How do you convince people who are strangers that you are worthy of their trust? When you apply the art of persuasion to the courtroom you begin to understand how to answer these questions.

Persuasion can be used for good or evil depending on the motivation or motivations of the person or persons seeking to persuade.[62] Also, as in all communication, the listeners' motivations are very important.

Review Chapter Four

- your reputation for truthfulness is your most important court-room assent

- know what you are talking about

- learn everything you can about your case and how cases work in general

- your job is to be understood, trusted and believed

- let the prosecutor make the arguments

- effective testimony is truthful testimony

- effective testimony is understandable testimony

- effective testimony is knowledgeable and therefore worthy of trust

- effective testimony draws its effectiveness from preparation

Review Questions

True or False

1. You should speak louder than you think is necessary.
2. You should speak slowly.
3. It is not proper to appeal to the jury's sympathy or emotion but it is proper to impress them with your knowledge.
4. It is the prosecutor's job to persuade the jury.
5. A truthful witness provides the best building blocks for a strong prosecution argument.
6. You should only raise your voice if the jury foreperson gives you a dirty look.

Multiple-Choice

1. Jurors are more readily persuaded by
   (a) likeable people
   (b) people who know what they are talking about
   (c) people who smell nice

   [ ]   All of the above
   [ ]   None of the above
   [ ]   (a) and (b)
   [ ]   (a) and (c)

2. Jurors will be more likely to trust you if you are
   (a) trustworthy
   (b) know your subject matter
   (c) a likeable person

   [ ]   All of the above
   [ ]   None of the above
   [ ]   (a) and (b)
   [ ]   (a) and (c)

3. It is perfectly ethical for a witness to
   (a) want the prosecution to win
   (b) slip a jury member a $20 (just in case)
   (c) avoid answering any question that contains the letter "q"

   [ ]   All of the above
   [ ]   None of the above
   [ ]   (a)
   [ ]   (a) and (c)

M/C   1. (a) and (b), 2. All of the above, 3. (a)
T/F   1. T, 2. F, 3. T, 4. T, 5. T, 6. F

CHAPTER FIVE
Courtroom Demeanor

> *Thus while he spake each passion*
>   *dimm'd his face,*
> *Thrice chang'd with pale ire, envy, and*
>   *despair;*
> *Which marr'd his borrow'd visage, and*
>   *betray'd him counterfeit ...*[63]
>
> — **Milton**
> (From *Paradise Lost*)

BODY LANGUAGE

Just relax. Be yourself. You have nothing to worry about. Unfortunately, it is easier to say relax than it is to be relaxed. I tell witnesses all the time "Just relax: you'll be fine." I don't know why I do this. If someone is nervous, probably the least effective way to help that person to relax is to *tell* him to relax. Yet, a relaxed witness *is* more effective than a nervous witness. How a witness acts and how a witness looks is almost as important as what he or she says. We ought to judge people impartially. We should listen to what a person says and judge that person on the logical coherence of his statement and the plausibility of his story[64] and not be unduly influenced by how he looks.[65] This, however, is not the world we live in.

This chapter takes into account how people judge other people in the real world. Every person is subject to bias and prejudice of one sort or another.[66] Most people are influenced by factors that are technically "improper."[67] The legal system sets up admirable, yet, unattainable goals for jurors.[68] Jurors are told to judge only on the facts of the case. Jurors are not supposed to permit any bias or prejudice to influence them. Yet, at the same time, jurors are the sole judge of the credibility of the witnesses.

> *We are born primed ... to attend to*
> *human faces and voices ... if say, we*
> *detect a mismatch between the words or*
> *tone of a person's speech and facial*
> *expressions or eye movements we may*
> *suspect deception.* [69]
> — **Brian Boyd**
> (From *On The Origin of Stories*)

It is well-known that people use mental short-cuts when judging others. We do not have time to get a person's life story when that person approaches us at 3 a.m. on a subway platform. We make quick (often incorrect) judgments about people based upon factors that are readily available to us at the time. We must decide if the person approaching us is a threat or harmless. Why? Because we cannot waste our time running or fighting every person we see. Therefore, we make snap judgments about a person based on how he looks, sounds, smells and moves.[70] We make these judgments often before that person even opens his or her mouth to talk—*if they talk at all.* Jurors are people. They judge the credibility of witnesses the way they would any person of whom they have little or no prior knowledge. Jurors are instructed to consider the facts and then later apply the law to those facts. It does not matter what the judge instructs the jurors to consider. A juror will size-up a person the way he or she has always done so. No legal instruction from a judge is going to change that fact.

> Speak loudly enough so that a person, who is sitting in the back of the courtroom, next to a loud clanking fan, who is hard-of-hearing, can hear what you are saying.[71]

Jurors are influenced (either consciously or subconsciously) by many factors: how a witness dresses; the manner in which he inflects his voice; whether she uses big or little words; whether he stutters or does not stutter; if rambles or speaks in paragraphs;

if he taps his feet and/or fingers or if he sits still; whether she speaks quickly or slowly loudly or softly; sits straight or slumps in her seat; acts polite or snarky; appears condescending or genuine; whether he makes eye-contact and if so to whom; if he smiles or doesn't smile; and yes, jurors will take notice if a witness appears nervous.[72] The above factors have little to do with the substance of a witness's testimony. Yet these factors do matter precisely because people (jurors) think they matter.[73]

> *... Avoid extravagant gestures.*[74]
> — **Cicero**

A large part of communication is nonverbal. When you testify, you testify with your dress, mannerisms, voice tone, eye contact, facial expressions and posture.[75] There are certain characteristics that communicate to people that you may be untrustworthy. Some of these characteristics may have nothing to do with your actual trustworthiness. Telling the truth is a necessary but not sufficient factor in effective testimony. You can tell the truth until the cows come home; however, if the jury doesn't believe you—it doesn't matter. In addition to telling the truth you also want to appear as if you are telling the truth.[76] Much like the Loch Ness Monster, there are some "Nesses" you should avoid when testifying.

NERVOUS*NESS* VS. CONFIDENCE

Nervousness is not a very accurate sign of untruthfulness.[77] Most studies show that nervousness is an unequi-vocal sign of—you guessed it—nervousness![78] Most people can clearly detect another person's unease. The

Avoid Tapping

signs of a person's nervousness include such physical attributes as fidgeting, sweating, verbal stammering, and lack of eye-contact.[79] Many studies show that these and other obvious signs of nervousness are conclusive prove that the person exhibiting these characteristics may or may not be telling the truth. I only make light of the fact that nervousness is not a very accurate sign of deception because it does not matter if nervousness is an accurate sign of deception. What matters is that many if not most jurors and judges *believe* that nervousness is an accurate sign of deception.[80]

> *"It's not exaggeration to say that our species owes its very existence to fear. But "unreasoning fear" is another matter.*[81]
> — **Daniel Gardner**
> (From *The Science of Fear*)

It is especially important, therefore, for the truthful witness like you to learn to control your nervousness. A good way to control the pre-testimony jitters is to be prepared.[82] Become thoroughly familiar with the process, your testimony, and what the prosecution expects of you. The more familiar you are with the entire process the more confident you will be.[83] Confidence is the flip-side of nervousness.

pHYsIcAL tIcS cAN bE dIsTRACtING

Each time you testify in court you will become less nervous. However, I assure you that you will always be a little nervous. The key is to control it.[84] Controlled nervousness is a good thing if it spurs you into action,[85] or if it causes you to prepare more thoroughly or concentrate better on what you are doing. Beyond this nervousness is wasted energy at best; at worst, many jurors see it as a sign that you are untrustworthy.[86]

A large contributing factor to pre-testimony nervousness is the fear of the unknown. Even if you have testified in court before, each case is different, and you can never be certain what questions you may be asked. Thorough preparation will never eliminate the uncertainties the courtroom but it can significantly reduce uncertainty.[87]

DEFENSIVE*NESS* VS. OPENNESS

Avoid the universally recognized posture of defensiveness: folded arms and a frown. If you exhibit a defensive posture jurors will think that you have something to hide. They will not trust you.[88] You can lose the trust of the jury simply by exhibiting defensive or slack mannerisms.[89] As confidence is the flip-side of nervousness, openness is the flip-side of defensiveness. Openness shows sincerity. You can exhibit openness, physically, by maintaining a natural posture. Just like it is easier to hit a 90-mph fastball if you maintain an easy, relaxed posture, it is easier to field a tough question if you maintain an easy, relaxed posture.

Most people know that their moods influence the way they look. But it is also true that the way you look can influence your mood. Even if you are not actually relaxed you can trick your body into believing that you are. Once your body thinks it is relaxed it signals to your brain that you are relaxed. The body influences the mind and the mind influences the body. This dynamic creates the opposite of a vicious circle. Battle your nervousness by faking calmness and equanimity.

COWARDLI*NESS* VS. VALOR

Your mom might have told you when you were a child to "sit-up" or "stop slouching." This was good advice then and it's good advice now.[90] I will change nothing except to say that you need to keep in mind that this does not mean that you should become stiff and ridged. You do not want to look like an escaped prisoner caught in the prison search light. Sit up straight but not stiff. Relax your muscles. Yes, literally relax your muscles. Consciously and deliberately relax your muscles as often as it takes for you to actually become relaxed. You can do this both before and as you are testifying. If you are relaxing your muscles properly it should be undetectable by the naked eye.

Smile when it is appropriate. However, smile only if it comes naturally to you. This advice really goes for most, if not all, of the demeanor-dos. If you are coming to the point in your testimony when you are about to describe the brutal pistol-whipping of the store clerk, by all means, frown, whimper, shake, whatever—my God, show some humanity! I must stress this point, do not smile if smiling doesn't come naturally to you. Some people cannot smile on demand. If smiling comes naturally go ahead and smile—except during the pistol-whipping part.

What are you to do with your hands? This is always a problem for people. You should try to keep your

Avoid Fidgeting

hands below the bench level, or below the level where the jury can see them. Try to keep them, like the rest of your body, rested and relaxed. The most important thing to remember about your hands is to keep them open at all times. Resist the urge to ball them into fists of fury. I have found that if I relax my hands when I testify the rest of my body seems to follow. If you must use your hands to speak, do so. Doing what comes natural to you trumps any of these guidelines as long as what comes natural to you is not inherently annoying or distracting. If you must use your hands to speak, like I do, try to keep them away from your face and try not to let your movements distract from what you are saying.[91]

> *... [When you speak] do not saw the air*
> *too much with your hand, thus, but use*
> *all gently: for in the very torrent,*
> *tempest, and, as I may say, whirlwind*
> *of passion, you must acquire and beget*
> *a temperance that may give it*
> *smoothness ...*[92]
> **— William Shakespeare**

EVASIVE*NESS* VS. DIRECTNESS

Just like openness is the positive side of defensiveness, directness is the positive side of evasiveness. We are often so used to being lied to by politicians and slick TV and Internet salespeople that we are shocked when the camera captures someone, who by all measures is supposed to lie to us, telling the truth without embellishment or spin. Jurors, like most people, expect to be lied to. Jurors do understand, however, that many people are probably less likely to lie while they are under oath and subject to the penalties of perjury. Yet witnesses lie. This part of the book is not about telling the truth verses telling lies. I assume that you are going to tell the truth. If you plan to lie on the witness stand, this book will be of no use to you.

> Make eye contact with the questioner when he/she asks the question. Make eye contact with the jury when you give your answer.[93]

This part of the book is about how to testify truthfully without looking like a liar. One of the best ways to look like a liar is to testify evasively. The best ways to appear trustworthy is to *be* trustworthy.[94] The second best way to appear trustworthy is to be direct. Shock the jury with your directness. Admit when you are wrong. If you made a mistake, do not make the defense attorney drag it out of you. Do not play word games. Just admit it. The jury will perceive you as more truthful if you readily admit your mistakes.[95]

Many completely honest witnesses answer cross-examination questions evasively because they think the questioner is out to "get" them. These people are correct. The cross-examiner *is* trying to get you. Answer straightforward questions directly. If you make it appear that you are trying to hide something, you are helping the cross-examiner achieve his or her goal. That is, you are helping him get you.

SERVILITY VS. POLITENESS

> *The principal officers of the empire were saluted, even by the sovereign himself, with the deceitful titles of your* **Sincerity** *your* **Gravity***, your* **Excellency***, your* **Eminence***, your* **sublime and wonderful Magnitude***, your* **illustrious and magnificent Highness***.*[96]
> — **Gibbon**
> (From *The Decline and Fall of the Roman Empire*)

I know what you are thinking: "What a great section!" It's true. I am the most enlightened, intelligent, illustrious, magnificent, honorable author in the world. You are honored simply by having the opportunity to read my wise and enlightened thoughts. Most people, however, are unlike me in that they are not magnificent in every way. Therefore, treat people with respect.

Always be polite. But never fawn or engage in insincere flattery. Most people can see through flattery and insincerity. It makes you look dishonest.

You should act in a manner that fits your surroundings. The courtroom is not a frivolous place. There are honors and traditions unique to the court setting. For example, everybody (including the judge) must rise when the jury enters or exits the courtroom. Traditions such as these serve to remind us that the courtroom is a serious place. If you must error, then error on the side of politeness. Just don't overdo it.

> "[Good speakers] control their eyes with great care.[97]
>
> — **Cicero**

How Do We Do It? Volume! Volume! Volume!

If you think you are speaking too loudly you are probably not speaking loudly enough. There are countless distractions that your voice must contend with, from the humming of the building's air conditioner to the noise of construction and traffic outside. Your voice also has to contend with internal distractions like juror boredom and hunger. If the prosecution chose to call you to testify before lunch—I have good news and bad news for you. The bad news is that most jurors will not be paying attention to what you are saying. The good news is that it probably doesn't matter. If the prosecutor put you on the witness stand to testify right before lunch, your testimony is probably not that important to the prosecution.

There are many exceptions to this rule. Last minute changes to the order of witness testimony are often unavoidable. This is because it is difficult to accurately estimate how long a person will be kept on the witness stand by cross-examination. Also, sometimes witnesses have unavoidable emergencies and the prosecution has to postpone his or her testimony. So, for reasons that are random and uncontrollable, you might move up or down in the batting order. Do not be offended if the prosecution calls you to the witness stand before lunch.

It is very common for an attorney to ask a witness an unfair or even outrageous question on cross-examination. Contrary to the popular notion that attorneys are supposed to ask questions that they themselves know the answer to, some attorneys may ask you to answer an outrageous question simply to rattle you. Frankly, the questioner doesn't know what your answer might be and doesn't really care. The only purpose of the question is to make you angry and defensive. Deprive him of his goal.

I will cover this topic in greater detail in the Cross-Examination Section. However, you should be aware from the beginning that you will not likely make it entirely through any testimony without somebody asking you a stupid or irrelevant or even infuriating question. Do not show the questioner or the jury that you are upset or annoyed. When you think a question is improper you should always pause momentarily to give the prosecutor an opportunity to object to the question. Do not, however, give the prosecutor a "help-me" look. Simply answer the question the best way you can. If you do not understand the question then that's your answer: "I do not understand the question."

Review Chapter Five [98]

Do

- smile (only if it comes naturally)
- sit upright relax your muscles (even if it does not come naturally)
- keep your hands open (even if it does not come naturally)
- breathe naturally (try)
- make eye contact with the questioner (even if it does not come naturally)
- give your answer to jury (depends on physical lay-out of courtroom)
- keep your hands away from your mouth (even if it does not come naturally)
- speak loudly (especially if this does not come naturally)
- try to relax (just try)

Don't

- Scowl
- Slump
- Sway
- Sigh (or)
- Slouch. [99]
- Tap
- Fidget
- Yawn or crouch.

Give no false praise and don't act aloof. If you do, at worst, the jury will think you are a liar; at best, they'll think you're a goof. Jury members will hold it against you if you appear evasive, hesitant, or exhibit physical tics such as twitching, stuttering, sweating, or blinking. [100]

Review Questions

True or False

1. Always complement the judge's robe.
2. Only roll your eyes if the defense attorney asks you a really, *really* stupid question.
3. Sit up straight like mama told you.
4. Always smile at the jury.
5. Always keep your hands away from your mouth while testifying.
6. Speak loudly.
7. Avoid playing word games with the questioner.
8. Just relax.
9. Be yourself.
10. Keep your hands open at all times.

Multiple Choice

1. If you are asked a question that annoys you by all means
   (a) show your disdain by twitching, stuttering and making duck sounds
   (b) respond by saying "That's an excellent question Your Exalted Eminence."
   (c) roll your eyes, look directly at the jury and silently mouth the words "I told you he is an idiot."

      [ ]   All of the above
      [ ]   None of the above
      [ ]   (a) and (b)
      [ ]   (a) and (c)

Fill-in the Blank

1. Avoid the universally recognized posture of defensiveness, _____ arms and a _____.
2. As openness is the positive side of defensiveness, directness is the positive side of _____.
3. Relax, you will be _____.
4. A large part of communication is _____.

FITB   1. folded, frown, 2. evasiveness, 3. fine, 4. non-verbal
M/C   1. None of the above
T/F   1. F, 2. F, 3. T, 4. F, 5. T, 6. T, 7. T, 8. T, 9. T & T, 10. T

CHAPTER SIX
Eyewitness Testimony

Things that Effect Your Ability to Perceive

- lighting conditions
- weather conditions
- duration of observation
- how far or close were you to the incident
- from what angle did you observe the incident
- was the scene moving or stationary
- was there anything blocking or partially blocking your view
- was there a time where you lost sight of the person or thing

---

In many cases the most important prosecution witness is the eyewitness. The prosecution may call you to testify as an eyewitness to any relevant action or omission (non-action) committed by the defendant or any other person.[101] The prosecution may also need you to testify as a circumstantial witness. The circumstantial witness can testify to actions by the defendant or another person that, along with other facts, prove the defendant's guilt or prove some other fact relevant to the case. An eyewitness may testify that he saw the defendant shoot the victim at point blank range and then flee down the alley. A circumstantial witness may testify that, although she did not actually see defendant shoot the victim, she did see the defendant running through the alley and observed him toss a handgun into somebody's backyard seconds after the victim was shot. For purposes of this section I will treat both the eyewitness and circumstantial witness the same.

The prosecutor is going to ask you questions that will highlight your three witness capabilities. First, the prosecution will try to show that you had the ability to perceive the events that you witnessed accurately. Second, the prosecutor will try to show that you can remember those events. You may be asked to remember events that your observed take place a long time ago. Third, the prosecutor will try to show that you can talk about these events now in a meaningful way. You need the ability to perceive, remember, and share your story.

There are as many factors that contribute to a witness's ability to perceive events accurately as there are events to be perceived. Every witness is different and every event witnessed is unique. However, there are some common questions that most witnesses are asked either as part of direct examination or cross-examination. Most good prosecutors will ask you questions that will show to the jury that your ability to perceive events is good and the circumstances under which you made your observation were optimal. If the circumstances were not optimal the prosecutor will ask you questions that bring about factors that existed that favor your ability to perceive events accurately in spite of the conditions. One of the first questions you should anticipate is what caused you to notice the event in the first place.

- ✓ There was nothing blocking my view.
- ✓ It was a clear sunny day.
- ✓ It was dark but it happened under the lamp post.
- ✓ I only saw the guy for a second but I'll never forget his face
- ✓ It was dark out but he was only a few feet away.
- ✓ I only saw him for a second but he ran right past me.
- ✓ He had a mask on but I'll never forget that voice.
- ✓ I would know that guy from anywhere he's lived in my neighborhood forever.
- ✓ It's not every day that someone points a gun at you; of course I remember the guy who did it.

What Was it About the Situation that Caused
You to Take Notice?

Be prepared to discuss with the prosecutor why what you observed was significant to you at the time of your observation. Why do you remember this particular fact among the countless facts that you have in your mind? It is not every day that you see a person pointing a gun at a clerk. That fact would obviously grab your attention. However, some observations are not obvious attention grabbers—except in hindsight. Why did you notice the defendant enter the bank? There is nothing strange about a person entering a bank. Maybe he wore a heavy coat on a hot day. Maybe he kept looking behind him. Maybe he paced back and forth three times before he finally entered the bank. Perhaps you noticed the defendant when he left the bank because he didn't just walk out the door—he ran like his pants were on fire. Maybe you saw the defendant shove a silver heavy object in his pants at the exact time a police officer entered the store.

These are examples of why one might have taken notice of a crime taking place. Many crimes (or circumstantial elements of crimes) are not obvious at the time of the initial observation. Even if your observation was not something as attention-grabbing as seeing a guy point a gun at a clerk, there is usually something out of the ordinary, even in seemingly innocuous behavior, that caught your attention. It is human nature for a person to become interested in something unusual in his environment. The prosecution will likely ask you to tell the jury why this event stuck out to you at the time is was occurring. If your interest is heightened at the time of the event, your motivation to perceive that event accurately is greater than if you were simply going about your day on autopilot.

It All Happened so Fast!

Time is the enemy of accurate perception. The prosecutor will likely ask you how you were able to accurately perceive something that happened so quickly. Did you have enough time to view and process what was going on? Did the actions develop slowly or were they quick and explosive? If what you witnesses happened quickly, how can you be sure your perceptions were accurate? Only you know the answer to these questions. It might be that, like what was discussed above, the incident was so unusual that, although fleeting, you will never forget what happened. The prosecutor might ask you how you were able to identify a defendant when the robbery happened so quickly. Many times a defendant might have a unique characteristic, like a tattoo, that although you only viewed for a second, was unmistakable. In

many cases the truthful answer is that you were not able to perceive every detail of the event accurately. In those cases there is
usually a detail or two that does clearly stick out in your mind.
Admit this and stick with the facts about which you are clear.

Weren't You Scared?

There are many factors that contribute to a witness's accurate
perception of events. There are some that both the defense and
the prosecution use to show that your ability to perceive events
were altered. Factors like anxiety, fear, nervousness, and excitement can affect a person's ability to accurately perceive events. In
addition to environmental stressors, such obvious factors as
alcohol or drug intake will affect your perception (also memory).
The anxiety-producing effect of crime is a popular topic of defense
assertions that a witness's perception is questionable.

It is normal for a person to suffer from anxiety while wit-
nessing a crime in progress. The question for lawyers is how does
anxiety affect witnesses' perceptions? The answer depends on who
you ask. The defense often contends that you could not have
perceived the events accurately because you were too scared. The
prosecution often contends the opposite. Because the event was
so traumatic, it was accurately burned into your brain. Who is
right? Who knows? It almost doesn't matter. The better question
is, "How did your anxiety affect *you*."

If you clearly perceived the person about whom you are
testifying, do not be intimidated by the defense attorney's cross-
examination about factors that might have affected your perception of the defendant. It is not important how those factors
might have affected you. It is only important how these factors
did affect you. You are not testifying about a theoretical observation but a real one. Only you know what you observed. However,
if you are not 100 percent sure about the person whom you
identified, by all means—say that! It is the nightmare of all moral
and ethical people to play any part in the conviction of an
innocent person. Aside from being a horrible injustice to the
person who is wrongly convicted, consider also, that the true
guilty party is presumably still free. This is a double injustice.
However, if you remember the event or detail accurately, then it
hardly matters if theoretically the average person might have a

difficult time accurately perceiving that same event or detail under those circumstances.

Details, Details, Details

The most telling cue that indicates what you observed is likely an accurate description of the person(s) or events that you describe is the volume and character of the details that you are able to describe. For example, if you observed an armed robber of a store clerk, what details are you able to remember about the suspect, victim, customers, and surrounding circumstances of the armed robbery? The number of details that you can accurately remember and describe makes a difference. The more details the better. However, the character of the factors that you remember and can describe accurately is important as well. In fact, it is often more useful to the prosecution for you to remember one unique detail of the armed robbery than for you to remember lots of vague notions of what happened. Consider the following statements given to police immediately following an armed robber of a convenient store.

Witness #1

> "I was standing by the Cheetos aisle, you know—where they keep the Cheetos and also the Nabisco products. I was like 6 feet away from the robber. I was looking over the Ho-Ho display, which was right next to a giant plastic Ho-Ho man; he must be some sort of character for the kids, like on TV. Anyway, it wasn't in my way or anything because the Ho-Hos were on sale and they weren't stacked up, high-like—you know, like they usually do on those displays. I saw a white guy pull out a gun and point it at the clerk. The clerk gave him money. Then the white guy just ran out of the store."

Witness #2

> "I was standing about 6 feet directly behind the guy with the gun. I noticed something was wrong when I heard him yell 'Open the drawer motherfucker! Now! Now!' I didn't see his face because I was directly behind him. I did see the

*gun. It was a black hand gun. A small gun. He had it in
his left hand. He wasn't wearing a mask or anything but I
couldn't tell you if he was black or white. He was very tall.
His voice was very weird though. He sorta sounded like—
his voice—like really, really deep—unusually deep; when
he ran out he seemed to favor his right leg—not a limp—
but sorta.*

Review Chapter Six

- you had the ability to perceive the events that you witnessed accurately

- lighting conditions

- weather conditions

- duration of observation

- how far or close were you to the incident

- from what angle did you observe the incident

- was it the scene moving or stationary

- was there anything blocking or partially blocking your view

- was there a time where you lost sight of the person

- you remember what happened

- you can talk about these events now in a meaningful way

- why was your observation significant at the time

- time is the enemy of accurate perception

- the number of details that you can accurately remember and describe makes a difference

Review Questions

True or False

1. You are more likely to remember an event accurately if that event happened quickly.
2. How anxiety affects the average person's ability to perceive events accurately is more important than how anxiety affects your ability to perceive events accurately.
3. The uniqueness of the details that you can describe accurately is more important than number of details you can describe accurately.
4. Internal states, like anxiety, fear, excitement, and depression, can have an effect on your ability to perceive, recall and relate events that you witnessed.
5. If you do not remember a detail or details say "I don't remember."

Multiple-Choice

1. Your ability to perceive the events that you witnessed accurately is affected by
   (a) internal states like anxiety, fear, excitement, depression
   (b) whether the scene you observed was stationary or moving
   (c) how much alcohol you had to drink at the time

   [ ]   All of the above
   [ ]   None of the above
   [ ]   (a) and (b)
   [ ]   (a) and (c)

CHAPTER SEVEN
A Few Rules of the Road

Prosecutors' cases consist of one thing, admissible evidence. What is admissible evidence? There are two general categories of evidence. These include physical evidence and testimonial evidence. Physical evidence is anything tangible. Physical evidence can include such things as clothing, weapons, blood, bullet fragments, stolen property, hand prints, etc. Testimonial evidence is witness or defendant testimony or statements. Depending on circumstances, these statements can be presented live, on video, through transcript, or read into the record by stipulation of the parties.

The question of what is *admissible* is greatly more complicated. The short answer to this question is that evidence is admissible *if the judge says it is admissible.* Judges are often incorrect. He or she may exclude evidence that is legally admissible; or he or she may admit evidence that is legally inadmissible. You can be an excellent witness for the prosecution and never know the difference. Many lawyers and judges do not know the difference. However, it is important for a witness, especially one who testifies often, to have a *general idea* of what the law permits. The rules of evidence are the rules of the road for trials.

Generally speaking you should leave the nuances of the law of evidence to the attorneys. The law of evidence is complicated and often contradictory. Listen to the question and answer the question. Let the judge decide what you should and should not answer. Always give the prosecutor a second or two to object to the defense attorney's question. If an attorney objects to anything, this includes the defense attorney, immediately stop what you are saying and wait for the judge to rule on the attorney's objection. Yes, stop mid-sentence if necessary. This is very important because what you say cannot be unsaid. You do not want to be responsible for causing a mistrial. What follows are some rules of evidence that affect witness testimony. When you hear an attorney object, it is probably because he or she thinks that one or more of the following rules of evidence were violated.

Q. What was the robber thinking at that time?

Objection!— Calls for Speculation

The Court: Sustained. Ask another question please.

A witness must testify about only those matters about which he or she has personal knowledge.[102]

Q. You went to where you heard the commotion because you wanted to see some action.

Objection! — Argumentative

The Court: Objection sustained.

Most people think an argumentative question is like a regular question only louder and meaner. This is not true. An argumentative question can be quite soft, even sweet. What makes a question argumentative is that the questioner is really not seeking an answer or otherwise doesn't care what your answer is. The questioner simply wants the jury take note of the question. It is really an argument disguised as a question.

Q. Tell me again how you were able to see my client when it was so dark.

Objection! — "Asked and Answered" and Argumentative

The Court: Sustained as to both objections.

The questioner only gets one bite at the apple. He or she cannot keep asking you the same question over and over again. The questioner can, and often does, get away with asking the sort-of same question in different ways. If you hear the words "tell me again," or "again," or "once more" or similar words or phrases— you probably already answered the question. In most cases "asked and answered" questions are also argumentative questions. They are usually argumentative in one of two ways. The questioner wants to highlight to the jury your answer because he thinks that your answer is favorable to his case. Another way in which an "asked and answered" question can also be argumentative is when you give the questioner an answer that he does not want. He will try to keep asking you the same question until (cows → home) the judge finally has enough or the opposing attorney objects and the court sustains the objection.

Q. When did you stop beating your wife?

> *Objection!—Argumentative and "Assuming Facts Not In Evidence"*

The Court: Sustained as to both objections. Be careful counsel!

Questioners are prohibited from incorporating "unproven" or "un-testified-to-already" premises with their questions. This question is also argumentative and probably irrelevant (depending on the case).

Q. When you spoke with the defendant was he sweating?

> *Objection!—Foundation*

The Court: Sustained

Which defendant (if there were more than one)? Which conversation; the one in the police car; the one on the street; the one when defendant was in lock-up? What time did this conversation take place? Who else was present? WHAT ARE YOU TALKING ABOUT?—BE MORE SPECIFIC. Otherwise, the witness has to speculate and will not be able to give a meaningful answer.

There are two very common objections that I purposely left out of this discussion. I left out the objection "question calls for *hearsay*" and the objection "question calls for an *irrelevant* answer." Many forests have been clear-cut to provide the paper for the books (before e-books were widely available) written about the topic of hearsay. If you can explain the intricate nuances of the hearsay rule, including its exceptions, in a couple of sentences, please write me and I will become your devoted follower.

I decided that you are better off letting the attorneys worry about what is or is not hearsay. The time this will free up in your schedule will permit you to plant that nice vegetable garden you always wanted to plant in your backyard. I did not discuss the concept of "relevance" (except for a quick mention) because relevance is very fact and case specific.

Review Chapter Seven

- testify only about those matters of which you have personal knowledge

- argumentative question is really an argument disguised as a question

- an asked and answered question is a question that the questioner has already asked you and (you guessed it) you have already given him or her the answer

- always give the prosecutor a second or two to object before answering a question

- rules of evidence are the rules of the road for trials

- a question is based upon proper foundation when it includes information that helps you to determine the *specific* matter upon which the questioner wants you to comment

- questioners often slip improper commentary into their questions

- questions that require you to explain what someone else was thinking are improper

Review Questions

True or False

1. An answer to a question is evidence.
2. Always pause a second or two before answering a question posed by the defense attorney.
3. Only testify to what somebody else was thinking if it is completely obvious.
4. The best way to handle an improper question is let the prosecutor object.
5. If the prosecutor's objection to a question is overruled by the judge you must answer the question whether you like it or not.

Multiple Choice

1. The following are foundational elements of a properly worded question
   (a) time
   (b) Krusty the Clown was the only other person in the room
   (c) location

   [ ]   All of the above
   [ ]   None of the above
   [ ]   (a) and (b)
   [ ]   (a) and (c)

M/C   1. All of the above
T/F   1. T, 2. T, 3. F, 4. T, 5. T

SECTION II
DIRECT EXAMINATION

Language and Word Choice

> *Do not let concrete melt into abstract ...*[103]
> — **George Orwell**

OUTLINE

> *Therefore, since brevity is the soul of wit, and tediousness the limbs and outward flourishes, I will be brief ...*[104]
> — **William Shakespeare**

OVERVIEW

The best speakers follow many of the same guidelines that the best writers use. Speaking and writing are different skills; however, they have a lot in common. The best speakers, like the best writers use simple words and they use them with precision. They say what they need to say without unnecessary words or phrases. They avoid using jargon. A good speaker consistently has his listener in mind. A good speaker's goal is to be fully understood.

Because giving testimony in a court of law is unique, many people believe that they have to completely change their manner of speaking. You do not. Well, not completely. The best testimony sounds natural. The best witnesses sound like they are having a natural conversation with the person asking the questions. These guidelines will make you seem more natural and less coached.

Most people do not use big words or technical jargon when they talk in everyday situations. Most people who desire to be understood know that they should be brief and precise.

CHAPTER EIGHT
Precision and Simplicity

> *Minds find more attractive what they can process more easily.*[105]
> — **Psychological Science**

The first step to being understood is to choose simple and precise words. Wherever you can decide between using a big word and a small one, use the small one. Sometimes this will not be possible. When you have a choice between simple phrasing and complex phrasing, choose simple. This does not mean that you need to dumb-down your testimony. That strategy will always backfire. Treat jurors like they are intelligent people. Ignorance is not the same as stupidity. Jurors will resent being treated like they are dummies. It is easy to strike a balance if you just answer the questions posed to you the way you would answer an intelligent friend if he asked you the same question.

EXAMPLE[106]

Q. [Radio did not give you plate number]?

A. No, it did not.

Q. Or any portion of a plate number?

A. No.

Q. You activated your emergency equipment?

A. Yes.

Q. As you would normally do in a routine traffic stop?

A. Correct.

Q. You approached the driver?

A. Yes.

Q. The window was already down?

A. That is correct.

Q. The driver did not attempt to flee?

A. No he did not.

Q. You had a brief conversation with the driver, correct?

A. That's correct.

Q. Asked for identification?

A. Yes.

Q. All in that order?

A. Yes.

The police officer in this example provided short, simple, direct, and appropriate responses. Short answers are generally better than long answers. This is especially true when you answer questions under cross-examination. Notice that the officer answered the question asked and only the question asked. He did not add anything or make gratuitous comment.

EXAMPLE

Q. What did you see the defendant do when you first arrived?

A. He left.

Just because your goal is to give simple and direct responses to simple and direct question it does not mean that you must leave stuff out or give vague answers. What does "he left" mean? He fled the scene? He took off running? He slowly faded off into a crowd of people? He began hitchhiking? If the answer is "He was gone when I got there." Then say "He was gone when I got there." However, if you saw him running east past the 7-11 knocking over old ladies and garbage cans over on his way ... then describe what you observed. This question called for a more detailed response.

EXAMPLE

Q. When you attempted to place handcuffs on the defendant what did he do?

A. The suspect refused to comply.

This answer is vague. What does "refused to comply" mean? Did defendant begin the engage you in a lengthy conversation about fish? Did he pull his arms away from you? Did he say "don't put those handcuffs on me or I'll kill you!" Did he stiffen up his arms to make it difficult for you to handcuff him? Refused to comply can mean many things. Give precise answers to open ended questions, especially when the question is being asked on direct-examination by the prosecutor.

EXAMPLE

Q. Describe what the defendant looked like when you first saw him get out of his car.

A. He was [Very] [Extremely] [Massively] drunk.

> *Some words are so vague they are essentially meaningless.* [107]
>
> — **Orwell**

This answer is poor for several reasons. First, words such as [Very] [Extremely] [Massively] are vague. They really do not say anything *specific* about your observation. Those words (and words like them) are really simply an expression of your emotional response to the facts, not an expression of the facts. Unless completely warranted (there are some *rare* instances where they are), don't use words that prop-up your testimony. These types of words usually add nothing to your testimony. Let the facts speak for themselves.[108]

EXAMPLE

A. Well [radio] related subject was armed with a black revolver.

Q. What significance does that have to you as an officer who is on patrol by yourself?

A. You never want to hear people are armed when you walk up to a car. It's very dangerous. When you do a traffic stop, the gun is probably the worst thing you could walk up on. So I was trying to be extremely careful.[109]

This is a good example of a police officer speaking is if he were a human being. This officer answered this question using regular everyday words: "car" *not* "vehicle," "armed" *not* "possessing a firearm," "walk up to a car," *not* "approach a vehicle," "probably the worst thing," *not* "creates a dangerous environment." Even the officer's use of the word "extremely" (which I normally discourage) seems apt in this context.

> **Avoid Using**
>
> "Quantum-Gibberish"
> (AKA "Mumbo-Dumbo;"
> AKA "Dr. Phil Speak.")
>
> These are phrases that contain big
> scientific-sounding words
> that have perfectly understandable
> English equivalents.

Review Chapter Eight

- favor simple words and phrases over complex ones

- favor short and direct responses *within reason*, never sacrifice precision

- avoid using jargon or cop-speak

- avoid using slang

- stay away from big scientific-sounding words

- use words and phrases that come naturally to mind; ones that you would use if you were telling a story to an educated friend

- when favoring the simple, remember also; do not talk-down to the jury

Review Questions

True or False

1. The best way to sound smart is to use big words.
2. Pronounce the number 9, Nine-ER.
3. Jurors love long, rambling, incoherent, irrelevant explanations concerning matters about which you were never asked.
4. Never answer a question in a manner that shows the people listening that you care about being understood.
5. People are mostly stupid so you always want to use very tiny words when testifying.
6. Because it is important for the jury to understand what you are saying always end every answer with the phrase "You dig?" or "Got that?"

Multiple Choice

1. The best way to say "I saw the guy crawl out of the red car and then stand-up" is
   (a) "when the said suspect alighted from the aforementioned vehicle I observed him couched almost prone, if you will. Then I fixed my department issued X4 Illumination device upon where suspect appeared to be crawling upon all fours, I noticed that, with great haste, he became ambulatory."
   (b) What's it to you?
   (c) "I saw the guy crawl out of the red car and then stand up."

   [ ]   All of the above
   [ ]   None of the above
   [ ]   (a) and (b)
   [ ]   (c)

CHAPTER NINE
Language, Jargon, Tone, Pronunciation, and Volume

> *Within your normal range, **a deeper voice is more persuasive. Your speech should be varied in volume, pace, rhythm and pitch. Monotone speech encourages sleep.**[110]*
> — Steven Wisotsky
> (From *Sounds and Images of Persuasion*)

AVOID PRETENTIOUS[111] LANGUAGE

Most people do not like a snob and a know-it-all, so avoid using overly technical words or unnecessary jargon.[112] All professions from law to architecture to medicine develop their own private languages. Members of these professions use words and phrases that are known to the in-group (other lawyers, architects doctors etc.) but unfamiliar to the out-group (everybody else). The purpose of your testimony is to inform your listeners, the judge or jury, in the most understandable way. This does not mean that you must speak like a two-year-old or talk down to your audience. Rather, use words that a normal educated person would use in everyday speech.

EXAMPLE

Q. What did you first notice about the defendant when you arrived on scene?

A. When I arrived the victim was not *ambulatory*.

The victim was not what? Sometimes you will have no choice but to use a medical or legal term. However, this is not one of those times. I cannot think of any reason to use the word "ambulatory." Just use regular words that you would use if you were telling a friend what you saw that day. [*Bob, you would not believe what I saw today. I drove right up on a traffic crash. I was*

71

the first one there. When I arrived I saw a woman in a red tee shirt hanging out of the drivers-side door. She was out cold. She woke up a few seconds later and pulled on the car door like she was trying to stand up, but she fell. She couldn't walk or move around.] In court you could not respond to the question *exactly* like the example above. You are not bound by the rules of evidence when talking with a friend. The part of the above response where you say "[she] pulled on the car door like she was trying to stand up" might draw an objection from the opposing attorney. Generally, a witness cannot testify to another person's intention based on that person's action (even when that intention is obvious). Nevertheless, you should still testify as if you were talking with an educated friend. Using big words and jargon will not make you immune from objections by the opposing attorney.

> *The difference between the right word and the wrong word is the difference between the lightning bug and the lightning.*[113]
>
> — **Mark Twain**

EXAMPLE[114]

Q. What did you do after you saw the defendant swerve in his lane?

A. *I curbed his vehicle.*

Please do not use this language in your answer. Ever! Thank you.

EXAMPLE[115]

Q. What did you see next?

A. Defendant *displayed* a blue steel handgun.

The word "displayed" is vague. Say what the defendant actually *did* with the gun.

EXAMPLE

Q. What did you do when you arrived at the crash site?

A. I spoke with the defendant who *advised* me that ...

To "advise" a person is to give that person a recommendation on a course of conduct or to give counsel. It can also mean to give someone information. It is better to just say, "I spoke with the victim and she *told* me ..." or "she *said*."

EXAMPLE

Q. What did she do with the credit card?

A. The purchases were placed on the victim's credit cards knowing that she was suffering from a mental impairment.

Passive voice is for politicians. You use passive voice whenever you do not identify the person doing the action. "Mistakes *were made*" instead of "*I* made mistakes." Police, prosecutors, and witnesses for the prosecution should limit their use of passive voice. Defendants and defense witnesses have an obvious interest in using passive voice. In some ways they are obligated to use passive voice. Defense attorneys and witnesses are expected to say, "the car was stolen" instead of saying "my client stole the car."

EXAMPLE[116]

A. Photos *were* placed into evidence ...

Who placed them into evidence?

EXAMPLE

Q. During your career [as a police officer] how many times have you seen firearms?

A. I have been *privy* to a lot of handguns.

Privy? Don't use this word, unless the question is "what word rhymes with "skivvy!"

EXAMPLE

Q. What information did you receive [before responding to offense]?

A. I received a radio message from my car commonly called an ISPERN message.

Q. What is an ISPERN message?

A. It's a statewide emergency radio network that a crime occurs in a neighboring town or somewhere in the area. You can use ISPERN to notify the other agencies in the area about any information you want.[117]

There will be occasions where it will be necessary for you to use specialized words or phrases that are known to people within the profession, but unknown to those outside the profession. These necessary words and phrases are called "terms of art." In the above example the prosecutor asked the officer about a particular type of message he received, so it was therefore necessary for him to use the term as it is used in the profession. However, notice that the officer was prepared to explain (and did explain) the meaning of ISPERN in simple language. Sometimes you have to use technical terminology because that term has a specific legal or medical meaning that cannot be better expressed with an everyday word. A medical doctor might testify that Bob suffered a "myocardial infarction." Nothing would be lost if the doctor testified, "Bob had a heart attack." Some terms are easier said in their specialized form. A doctor testified to the following, "The first thing I did was order the nurse to give Jack an IV of very strong antibiotic." The term "IV," even though a medical term, is probably the best choice. It would be unwieldy for the doctor to use simpler non-medical words.

I ordered nurses to administer a bag that hangs on a metal poll that often, but not always, uses the power of gravity to administer liquids, most often saline (that is salt) which drips down a tube to a patient entering through that patient's vein.

EXAMPLE

Most often specialized words or phrases are unnecessary. A simple plain English word or phrase will do just fine.

Q. ... [Detective] what did you do next?

A. I responded to Christ Hospital in Oak Lawn where both victims had been transferred by CFD ambulances.

Q. What was your purpose for going to Christ Hospital that night?

A. To check on the condition of the two subjects who had been shot....

A. When I got to the hospital I found that [victim] had been pronounced DOA on arrival ...

Q. When you say DOA, is that dead on arrival?

A. Dead on arrival.[118]

In the strict sense, "DOA," like "IV," is not a technical medical term but an abbreviation. The fact that professionals use an abbreviation or phrase in the course of their employment does not make it a "term of art." Generally, it is better to use a phrase than an abbreviation of a phrase. If there is any chance that the abbreviation you use will be either misunderstood or not understood by your audience then say the words themselves. For instance, CFD means Chicago Fire Department: not everybody knows this. DOA means dead on arrival: not everybody knows this (although I suspect DOA is more widely known than CFD). You do not have to go overboard with limiting abbreviations. It is perfectly acceptable, for example, to say "FBI" or "USA." Let your common sense dictate your choice of words in this area.

EXAMPLE

Q. He was walking toward you and saying, "Get out of my house"?

A. Correct.

Q. And from *that* you thought he was going to hit you?

A. I didn't know if he was going to hit me, grab me, whatever; it put me in reasonable fear of receiving a battery.

The phrase "reasonable fear of receiving a battery," is the definition of the crime of assault. Never use statutory language in your answer! It makes you look like someone who knows what to say in order to win. It is not a natural way of speaking and it makes you look dishonest.

MORE JARGON, COP-SPEAK, IMPRECISE, AND VAGUE LANGUAGE[119]

She took the *stated funds* ... = [She took the money.]

The victim stated that as she was walking toward her car a male white *who was described* to be stocky build wearing a red tee shirt ... = [Who described this person?]

After the incident occurred, victim drove to her boyfriend's house who *resides* in Chicago ... = [What incident? Be more specific. For example: after the defendant shot the victim. Also, the boyfriend *lives* in Chicago.]

I affected a traffic stop ... = [Pulled over the van.]

On arrival *I was advised* by Officer Gomez that a male white *subject* wearing a teal shirt *who was involved* in the disturbance *could possibly* be in the area *and needed to be located* for questioning ... = [Officer Gomez told me ... *subject* = unnecessary ... What did this male white person do to make him *involved*? When you use the word *could* you do not need the word *possibly*. Needed to be located should be = Officer Gomez told me to find him.]

... *was positively identified* as cocaine by ... the cocaine *substance* and rolled up dollar bill *was placed* into evidence ... = [Who positively identified the cocaine? If you say *cocaine* you do not have to say *substance*. *Who* placed the cocaine into evidence?]

Other police units searched the area with *negative results.* = [Unless you are a medical professional talking about the *specific results* of a *specific blood test*, do not say negative results.]

I *exited* my squad car and approached the *vehicle* on the passenger's side. = [I walked to the passenger's side of the blue van.]

I used my *department issued flashlight to illuminate* the inside of the *vehicle* ... = [What?]

... that is where *I located* a metal pipe *used for ingesting* cannabis ... = [I found a metal pipe in the glove compartment of the car. It was the type of pipe that people often use to smoke cannabis.]

... after taking the GPS unit, *she then alerted Omar of her presence* ... = [How? Did she call him on her cell phone? Hand signal? Smoke signal? How?]

GPS unit *was recovered* and Omar *was taken* into custody. = [I took the stolen GPS from his hand and arrested him; or arrested Omar; or arrested the defendant.]

I was in the *immediate vicinity* of victim's *residence* when the call came out ... = [I was near victim's house when ...]

GOOD DETAIL AND USE OF EVERYDAY WORDS AND PHRASES

A. ... then I saw the offender jack-up the red van while it was still in the driveway ... he removed the lug nuts and took off the passenger's side front tire ... I saw him fishing through the tire's open slots. He pulled out a small screwdriver and broke the tire lock; I heard it pop ... a pop or cracking sound ... I was right there almost standing next to the guy ... Then he just took off...

Q. What happened once you searched the car?

A. Opened up the driver's door, and the first thing I noticed was an unusual bump below the steering wheel. I pulled on the plastic piece that was jutting out and the butt of a gun fell out.

PRONUNCIATION, VOLUME AND VOICE TONE

In Chapter 4, I address the topic of courtroom demeanor. Pronunciation, volume, and voice tone is a subset of demeanor. However, because the quality of your voice, for better or worse, is the vehicle by which you assault or soothe your listener's ears, it deserves its own chapter. The common wisdom of the courtroom dictates that you speak slowly *and* loudly. This is only half right. You *do* need to speak loudly. You *do not* need to speak slowly. It is necessary for you to speak loud enough so that the entire courtroom can hear what you are saying. If you think you are talking too loudly, then you are probably speaking at the correct volume. Your voice competes against countless distractions, both external and internal. External distractions include talking in the audience, hallway, construction, or street noise, and countless other auditory distractions.

You also compete with internal distractions that plague even the most studious listener. These include hunger, boredom, heat, cold, uncomfortable chairs, problems at home, short attention spans, etc. You must never cause the judge or jury to strain to hear what you are saying, they won't. A myth that almost every lawyer believes is that witnesses should speak slowly if they want their audience to believe what they are saying. This may be simply a natural, but incorrect, inference from people's common experience. Fast talkers are the used car salespeople of the world. These are the people trying to sell you something. People who speak fast are attempting to trick you somehow. All of this is true. However, it is also true that confident and knowledgeable people often speak quickly. If you are confident in what you are saying there is more danger in artificially slowing your speech than there is danger in speaking at your normal pace. Subject to a couple of exceptions noted in this chapter, you should strive to speak as naturally as possible.

> *Don't be afraid to pause especially when you want to punctuate an important point.*[120]
> — **Antonin Scalia**
> (From *Making Your Case*)

I can't overstate the importance of using a loud voice and a natural well-paced delivery. There are times when commonsense will dictate that you slowdown or speedup your delivery. There are times when, for emphasis, it is advisable for you to use a strategic pause.[121] A pause in your speech can be an effective way to emphasize an important point or signal a transition in what you are about to say. Think of a strategic pause as sort of a verbal paragraph break.

Your voice tone should have natural variance.[122] Not every question will have the same emotional impact or attract the same level of interest in your response. Your voice tone will change without you having to think about it much. The volume of your voice will take conscious effort for some witnesses.

COMMONLY MISPRONOUNCED COURT WORDS

Defend*ant*[123]

[Like a family picnic, defend"ant(s)" can spoil a good time. That's why you should pronounce this word defend "int(s)."]

De*fense*[124]

[When speaking in court, you should erect a fence to defend your position. That's why you should always stress the "fense" in defense.]

Ca*l*m[125]

[Please stay "Kahm" when I tell you this fact; do not pronounce the "L" in calm.]

Con fiscate[126]

[As any con knows there is no "com" in confiscate.]

En *route*[127]

[While en route to the scene of the crime, you should always think about the ROOT of the problem; because without a doubt, you never pronounce en (root) in-ROWT.]

Jur*or*[128]

[Jurors won't know what your testimony is for if you pronounce jur-"ur" like jur-"or."]

Juve*nile*[129]

[If you want to be young again and mistake free then a river is not a place you want to be. Until you are old enough to visit a river in Africa, *stay away* from any juve-"anul" who thinks juve-"nile" rhymes with "pile."]

WORD AND PHRASE PITFALLS

There are a lot of words and phrases that we all use as a matter of habit or laziness. Most are perfectly acceptable outside the context of a court trial. When you testify every word counts. The judge and jury do not know you and, therefore, will not necessarily give you the benefit of the doubt when you say something that "comes across wrong." Many people use phrases and words that make them appear dishonest, evasive, or simply uneducated.

Avoid Using These Words and Phrases[130]

"To be honest with you ..."	Use only if you were lying to the judge and jury the entire time and you are just now coming clean.
"Actually ..."	Like "to be honest with you" use only if you were lying to the judge and jury the entire time and you are just now coming clean.
"To tell you the truth ..."	Do you want a medal? You are supposed to tell the truth. Please don't say this. I beg of you!
"*We* saw the suspect ..."	Answers that contain the pronoun "we" are rarely correct. Unless the questioner *specifically* asks you what you *and* your partner did or saw next (which is an improper question), you should not say "*we* did," "*we* saw," "*we* arrested," "*we* chased," etc. The appropriate response is "I did," "I saw," "I arrested," "I chased," etc.

"sort of" "it looked like" "around" "maybe" "I think" "it seemed like" "I kind of thought"	These are hedge words and phrases. They make your testimony look weak. Many people use hedge words even when they are certain of what they are saying because they do not want to appear arrogant. In court, if you are certain of what you are saying, do not use these types of verbal hedges. Only use them when you are truthfully uncertain. Do not use them to be polite.
"extremely" "definitely" "massively" "surely"	These words are called intensifiers. Use intensifiers sparingly. It is okay to use words and phrases that show certainty. However, in most (not all) cases, you do not need to modify your words to make them stronger. Let your observations speak for themselves.
"umm," "ah," "ya know"	Try to avoid verbal tics. They are distracting.
"Folks," "yah all"	Avoid language that is too familiar, slang, first names, colloquialisms, unless completely appropriate based on the context of the question asked. (If the prosecutor asks you, "What did you say when the guy entered the store?" And the truthful answer is, "Oh Fuck! That guy has a gun!" You should say exactly that.)
"The Honorable Exulted" "Sir-yes-sir!" "That's an excellent question!"	Don't kiss butt. It is obvious. It makes you look dishonest.

EXAMPLE[131]

Q. What kind of materials did they provide you?

A. Basically reports, case files, and evidence.

Q. OK. Now the word "evidence" could be somewhat broad. Can you be a little more specific?

A. Weapons, shell casings, rape kits, photographs. *To be honest with you* I *actually*—I personally—was not involved in the taking of any evidence...

This officer "actually" used "to be honest with you" and "actually" in the very same sentence!

EXAMPLE[132]

Q. When you spoke to [mother and fourteen-year-old daughter] did you speak to them together or separately?

A. Both actually. (There is that word again—please do not use the word "actually.")

Q. Could you explain that?

A. I spoke to them together at the beginning, and then decided to speak to [fourteen-year-old girl] separately because she was a young girl. I think at the time she was fourteen. We wanted to make sure that she had an independent recollection of what happened, that she wasn't just regurgitating what her mother just said.

The above explanation is very good. (Except for the word "we," always testify to what "you" did, unless the question clearly calls for a "we" response.) Whenever you have an opportunity to demonstrate truthfully that you conducted your investigation in a manner that maximized the accuracy of the information, do so. There are probably countless ways that you do this in your investigation, ways that you may not even be aware of. Make sure that you discuss this in detail with the prosecutor before you take the stand.

Review Chapter Nine

- most people don't like snobs or know-it-alls

- avoid overly technical words or unnecessary jargon

- use words that a normal educated person would use in everyday speech

- speak at your normal pace (within reason)

- use natural pauses

- speak with the deepest voice that comes naturally to you

- allow your speech to vary in tone volume like it would naturally unless you naturally speak with a whisper

- avoid using slang overly familiar words or phrases unless necessary as part of a truthful answer

- avoid using hedge words and phrases unless necessary as part of a truthful answer

- only testify to what you saw with your own eyes, heard with your own ears or felt with your own senses

Review Questions

True or False

1. Speak louder than you would normally speak unless you normally speak loudly.

2. Within your natural range a deeper voice is better.

3. Use natural pauses.

4. If you naturally speak like a robot, change the way you speak when you testify.

5. It is advisable to use the phrase "to be honest with you" only if the phrase is also the name of a bar and you were responding to the question, "What is the name of that bar—you know—the one with the weird name?"

6. The best and probably only appropriate circumstance in which you should say the word "actually" is when opposing counsel screams at you "Liar! Liar!" It is appropriate for you to respond "Actually, sir, my pants are not, in fact, on fire."

7. It is always a good idea to call the judge "Your Highness."

8. When you are not sure about an answer to a question the most appropriate answer is "I am not sure."

9. When you are certain about something it is better to say "It seemed like" or "I think," because you do not want to appear arrogant.

Multiple Choice

1. You are the victim of an armed robbery. When the robber
   confronted you at the cash register he said; "Let me see your
   motherfucking hands—now! Put 'em up, bitch!" The prosecutor asks you on direct examination, "What, if anything did
   the defendant say to you?" (Assume prosecutor otherwise laid
   proper foundation for question.) What is the correct answer to
   this question?

   (a) He said, "Let me see your motherfucking hands—now! Put
       'em up, bitch!"
   (b) He told me to put up my hands.
   (c) He wanted to see my hands so he told me to put them up.

   [   ]   All of the above
   [   ]   None of the above
   [   ]   (a) only
   [   ]   (b) only
   [   ]   (c) only

2. Same question #1, except that it is the defense attorney
   asking the question on cross-examination.

   [   ]   All of the above
   [   ]   None of the above
   [   ]   (a) only
   [   ]   (b) only
   [   ]   (c) only

M/C   1. (a) only,   2. (a) only

SECTION III
CROSS-EXAMINATION

> *In all criminal prosecutions, the accused shall enjoy the right ... to be confronted with the witnesses against him.*[133]
> — **U.S. Constitution**
> Amendment VI

OUTLINE

OVERVIEW SECTION III

In 1980, the United States Supreme Court stated again the commonly held view that the aim of our judicial system is the pursuit of justice. Justice White wrote, "There is no gainsaying that *arriving at the truth* is a fundamental goal of our legal system."[134] Courts have long maintained that the proper functioning of our adversary system depends on proper and effective cross-examination in an attempt to elicit the truth.[135] If each side subjects the other's witnesses to the crucible of cross-examination, somehow, the truth will emerge.[136] The United States Supreme Court has also recognized the vital role that cross-examination plays in providing the defendant, and indeed the prosecution, the right to a fair trial.[137] This right has deep roots in our common law system and is reflected in our constitution.[138] The Confrontation Clause of the Sixth Amendment of the United States Constitution provides that: "In all criminal prosecutions, the accused shall enjoy the right ... to be confronted with the witnesses against him."[139]

Because of these and other justifications, cross-examination is a large part of the trial process. In this section you will learn the function of cross-examination and its objectives. The more

87

acquainted you are with how attorney's use cross-examination, the better you will be at answering questions posed by adverse parties. Once you have understanding of the general uses and purposes of cross-examination you need to prepare for this type of questioning for a specific case—your case. Chapter Thirteen teaches how one ought to specifically prepare for cross-examination for a specific case. The final chapter provides tips for surviving cross-examination.

CHAPTER TEN
Main Objectives of Cross-Examination

Most people know what cross-examination looks like. Cross-examination is usually the part of the movie where the hero attorney, fighting against the seemingly indestructible weight of the state and all of its bottomless resources; fighting alone; armed with only his wit, an unpaid law clerk, and the courage to fight an unwinnable fight for a lost cause; forces a key prosecution witness to breakdown on the witness stand and admit—"It was all a big lie! A big lie! We set up your client to be the fall guy! Your client is innocent!" I love this part of the movie. This rarely happens in real life. But that is why you go to the movies; to escape from the drudgery and monotony of real life. At its most basic level, cross-examination is simply a way of asking questions. Attorneys are permitted to ask leading questions (questions that suggest the answer; "Isn't it true," questions) when cross-examining a witness. It is a very important part of our adversarial system. But let us not fool ourselves; there is nothing magic about cross-examination. Even the best cross-examiners are unlikely to ever get someone to breakdown on the witness stand like the fictional TV and movie lawyers. Cross-examination follows direct examination. Generally, attorneys are not permitted to ask *leading* questions on direct examination of a witness.

Evidence Tip

FEDERAL RULES OF EVIDENCE – RULE 611

In Chapter Three of this book we looked at Federal Rule of Evidence 611 (a). Even though Rule 611 (a) governs cross-examination (not the express subject of Chapter Three), I think it is important that you learn early and often not to fear cross-examination. Below is Rule 611 in its entirety.

(a) **Control by court**.

The court shall exercise reasonable control over the mode and order of interrogating witnesses and presenting evidence so as to (1) make the interrogation and presentation effective for the ascertainment of the truth, (2) avoid needless consumption of time, and (3) protect witnesses from harassment or undue embarrassment.

(b) Scope of cross-examination.

Cross-examination should be limited to the subject matter of the direct examination and matters affecting the credibility of the witness. The court may, in the exercise of discretion, permit inquiry into additional matters as if on direct examination.

(c) Leading questions.

Leading questions should not be used on the direct examination of a witness except as may be necessary to develop the witness' testimony. Ordinarily leading questions should be permitted on cross-examination. When a party calls a hostile witness, an adverse party, or a witness identified with an adverse party, interrogation may be by leading questions.[140]

RECOGNIZING CROSS-EXAMINATION OBJECTIVES

Good cross-examiners will often begin their questioning by asking you to admit certain facts that both sides agree with. This is the friendly part of cross-examination. There are many reasons an attorney might start out asking you questions about matters that are uncontested. First, this type of questioning gets your relationship off on a friendly footing. Starting out friendly makes the questioner seem reasonable and likeable. Also, by asking you to admit to facts that you agree with, he will get you used to saying "yes." He will develop a rhythm of yes. This will cause *you* to break the rhythm when the questions become harder. A good cross-examination, from the cross-examiner's perspective, always puts the focus on the witness. That means that if the attorney questioning knows what she is doing, she will not likely begin her cross-examination by yelling at you. The beginning of an effective cross-examination, aside from leading questions, sounds very much like an effective direct examination.

There are even more nefarious reasons for starting out friendly. Sometimes an attorney will ask a seemingly friendly question as a *set-up* for a not so friendly question regarding the same topic later. He or she might be attempting to *lock you into a position* that you will later regret. This is one of the many reasons to tell the truth. There is an old saying that goes like this, **Tell The Truth: It's Easier to Memorize.**

Not all friendly questions are "set-up" questions. Often, attorneys will ask witnesses to affirm uncontested facts to simply get those facts out of the way. Some attorneys, typically prosecutors, prefer to narrow the issues.[141] If the opposing attorney believes that your testimony has not hurt his case, he may ask you a few simple, friendly questions and sit down. In some cases, when the opponent thinks you have not hurt (or actually helped) their case, he will ask you no questions at all. This technique is more common for the prosecution than the defense. The defense usually will ask at least some questions so that he may use your testimony in a later appeal.[142]

SHORT REVIEW OF CROSS QUESTIONS

Questions asked by the attorneys are not evidence. Answers are evidence. The jury may choose to believe, disbelieve, or disregard any answer to any question as long as the judge permits that answer to stand. This does not stop cross-examiners from trying to make points with the jury by their questions alone. All trial lawyers know the old legal maxim "never ask a question (on cross-examination) that you do not know the answer to." Like many other sayings of common wisdom this is not true. Notwithstanding: "questions are not evidence"; often attorneys will ask a question simply for the purpose of having the jury hear the question. In other words the attorney asking the question doesn't care what answer is. Even if the question turns out to be improper or otherwise struck from the record—the jury already heard the question—you can't *un*-ring the bell. The judge can instruct the jury to disregard the question. A judge's order to disregard is about as effective as my request in the following sentence. Do not read the next sentence please. *My favorite fruit is mango.* You read the sentence anyway—didn't you? Mangos anybody?

TYPICAL QUESTIONS: TYPICAL TOPICS

You May Be Asked Questions That Are Calculated to (Show):

1. ***Support Defense Theory***[143]
       AKA
   "I-Should-Have-Called-You-As My-Witness-Cross"

Q. Isn't it true that you saw Mr. Jones hit my client first?

_____

Q. When you inventoried the victim's property he had a silver cell phone in his pocket—true?

Q. My client could have mistaken that cell phone for a gun isn't that correct?

_____

Q. You never saw my client before you pulled him over for DUI?—you don't know him?

Q. You testified that he had slurred speech; you don't know how he normally speaks—right?

_____

Q. It was very dark in the alley where you were robbed isn't that true?

_____

Q. The first person you arrested—the one you let go—she also had braided black hair like my client—true?

2. ***That You Are Ignorant of Certain Important Facts***
       AKA
   "That's-Interesting: Now-Can-We-Talk-About-Something-That-Matters-Cross"

Q. You testified that you witnessed my client running from the alley holding a gun—correct?

Q. You never actually saw my client shoot that gun isn't that correct?

_____

Q. You testified that you inventoried victim's belongings after he was shot—right?

Q. You said on direct [examination] that the phone was "silver" or "silvery" in color—true?

Q. My client told police that the victim pointed a black gun at him?

Q. Isn't it true that you have no idea what victim's "silver" cell phone might have looked like pointed at my client in a very dark alley?

_____

Q. You saw my client enter the _Sack O Suds_[144] convenient store, correct?

Q. Five minutes later you saw him exit? Isn't that correct?

Q. You did not see what my client was doing inside the _Sack O Suds_?

_____

3. *That You Are Uncertain About Important Facts*

Q. You said that the robbery took place approximately 1 a.m. isn't that correct?

Q. You were not staring at a clock at the time of the robbery—right?

Q. The robbery could have taken place at 1:30 or even 2 a.m. as far as you know? Right?

_____

Q. You said that my client had been drinking all night at _DUI Bar & Grill_?

Q. This is allegedly what the passenger of the car told you—right?

Q. You did not actually see my client drink anything that night did you?

Q. You have no idea, outside of what somebody else told you, someone who was herself drinking, where my client had been before you pulled him over?

---

4. *That You Are Biased*

Most people who testify for either the prosecution or the defense are biased. There is nothing wrong with bias. If you are a police officer you should never have to make the following statement to your therapist:

Police Officer: "Doctor, the guilt is killing me. My whole career I have been living a lie."
Doctor: Yes. Yes. Go on."
Police Officer: (Whimpering hands over his face.) "OK. Here goes. Doctor, I have always hated criminals! There I said it! I don't know why, but ever since I was a young boy I have had a strong dislike of people who victimize other people! CAN YOU HELP ME, doctor?

Improper bias is bad. Bias is improper when it rests on an irrelevant fact or facts. Improper bias clouds your judgment in a way that causes you to overemphasize irrelevant facts or underemphasize relevant facts. Racial, gender, ethnic and religious biases, for example, are improper *and* irrelevant. There are many obvious reasons why it is a bad idea to bring improper bias to the witness stand. Although not as important as the obvious moral reasons to avoid improper bias, improper bias makes you an unreliable witness.

A person who has a racial bias, for example, is more likely to focus his or her attention on factors that have little to do with the crime. They commit the errors in judgment and perception that I mentioned in the third sentence of this paragraph (overemphasizing irrelevant facts; or underemphasizing relevant facts). Improper bias can include bias that may naturally arise when a witness has a personal interest in the outcome of a case. If, for example, you stand to gain a financial or other type of personal benefit from the defendant's conviction for the crime charged. The defense will know about any personal interest in the outcome of the case before you hit the witness stand. The prosecution must disclose this to the defense. If you have personal interest in the outcome of a criminal case other than the desire to see the truth told and/or justice served, you probably should not testify. Theoretically, a person who has a personal stake in the outcome of a case can tell the truth. But I'm not buying it. Do not be afraid to admit proper bias! Do not let improper bias filter its way into the court record. Let the facts and not personal feelings determine the outcome of the case.

5. *That You Have Some Motive to Lie or Exaggerate*
AKA
"Pants-On-Fire-Cross"

Q. You testified that you observed the defendant drinking all night at *DUI Bar & Grill*—correct?

Q. You are aware that defendant owns the *DUI Bar & Grill* aren't you?

Q. You just so happen to own *Treachery Bar & Grill* down the street. Right?

Q. So you stand to make money if my client loses his liquor license and goes out of business. Isn't that correct?

———————————————————

Q. You testified that the robbery took place at 1 a.m. Isn't that correct?

Q. You are sure about that time—right? You're sure about the time because the robbery took place immediately after you left the bar—after the bar closed. True?

Q. *Treachery Bar & Grill* closes—it closes at 1 a.m.—true?

Q. There is a place across the street that is open all night, right?

Q. If you were in fact robbed at *3 a.m.*, you would have to explain to your wife that the only business open at *that* time is the *Motel Infidelity*? You couldn't have been leaving *that* business because you are married—true?

---

6. *Confront You with Your Own Statements*

Q. You testified about this matter in a preliminary hearing?

Q. At the preliminary hearing you said you didn't remember what time you were robbed—true?

Q. Yet today you are sure that you were robbed at 1 a.m. Correct?

Q. After you pulled over my client, that night, when the events were fresh in your mind, you wrote a report about this incident—correct?

Q. Today you testified that my client "could barely walk, was stumbling all over the place," correct?

Q. Nowhere in your report do you mention that my client could barely walk or was stumbling isn't that true? We are hearing those words for the first time today.

A favorite defense tactic on cross-examination of a law enforcement witness is to point out what is *not* in the report. Even though reports are simply summaries of events and not comprehensive word-for-word accounts of the events that they describe. No person could include every possible detail in every report. Notwithstanding this fact, you should attempt to be as detailed as possible in your reports.

Another favorite defense tactic is to cross-examine you about an observation that you did not include in one report but did include in another. A related tactic is for the cross-examiner to refer to absence of a fact in one part of a report, when you included that fact in a different part of the same report. Read your reports thoroughly before you testify! If you know the contents of your reports these tactics will come up cold.

7. *What You Clearly Could Have Done—but Did Not Do AKA* *"Woulda-Coulda-Shoulda-Cross"*

This is the most popular cross-examination technique employed against law enforcement officers. Impeachment by omission can be effective no matter how thoroughly you conducted the investigation. This is especially true in times of budget tightening. You can conduct an effective and thorough investigation with limited resources and limited manpower. You cannot conduct a perfect investigation. In a world of possibilities you can't chose them all. Everything you did will be measured against everything you could have theoretically done but didn't. The benefit of hindsight makes this a very effective cross-examination technique. Unless you did everything, and you didn't; unless you thought of everything, and you didn't; your investigation was fatally flawed. The "real killer" is somewhere out there—and it's all your fault. "Woooda-Coulda-Shoulda-Cross" comes in many varieties. The following are just some examples:

Phantom Witness Syndrome

Q. If you talked to witness A and witness B, why didn't you attempt to discover if witness C exists; and if so, if witness C knows anything about who actually killed the victim?

Q. Isn't it true, officer, that you failed to even look for—let alone talk to—defendant's alibi witness?
A. What alibi witness?

Q. Didn't my client tell you that he was with somebody the whole time between 6 p.m. and 6 a.m. on the night of the shooting?
A. Yes.

Q. You didn't even bother questioning that person did you?
A. No.

Q. Too busy framing my client!

OBJECTION!

The Court: Sustained.

Q. Your client told me he was with a guy. He thinks the guy's name is Frank or Bob or something. Your client said he thinks Frank or Bob lives in Detroit or Québec, but he's not sure. No. No, I did not question every person named Frank or Bob who lives in the Greater Detroit—or Québec—metro areas.

Q. Do you know a person who they call "Silky Sam the Guitar Man"?
A. No

Q. No further questions.

Sometimes attorneys, stricken with "Phantom Witness Syndrome," will simply invent a name of a person. Then he will ask you if you know that person; then just leave the question "out there" to percolate around in the minds of the jurors. "I wonder who 'Silky Sam the Guitar Man' is?" "He must be somebody important." "I wonder why the detective didn't question *him*." "I bet he's the real killer." (Juror speculation does all the work for you (if you are the defense attorney).

Completely Unnecessary Test Anxiety (Cu-ta)

Q. You testified that you observed my client leaving the store without paying for the item, correct? You arrested him outside the store—why didn't you take a DNA sample? He was right there—he would have consented.

Q. I know that after you pulled my client over for DUI he agreed to take a breathalyzer and failed, correct? Why didn't you also have my client give a blood, urine, and hair follicle sample for spectral-geo-titular-hydrogen-heavy-proton[145] analysis?

Q. You tested the gun and my client's extremities and clothing for gunshot residue, right? But you did not even bother testing my client's trigger finger—did you?! Did you?!

Q. Officer, you testified that you were off duty when you observed my client rob the bakery at gunpoint—true? Are you aware that the French recently developed a machine that can accurately detect if a person has been exposed to bread crumbs? You didn't even bother to run that test did you?

Unnecessarily Lazy Investigator Exhaustion (U-LIE)

Q. You say you searched the crime scene where the victim's body was found—correct? She was found on a bench in the park—right? But you didn't search the Museum of Science and Industry, did you?

Q. You testified that you and your partners canvassed the area—correct? Oh, I see, but you didn't canvass what was not in the area—did you? You didn't have time! You wanted to go home and watch the Chicago Bears!

Q. You testified that you searched my client for officer safety isn't that right? For weapons—guns, knives, and such, correct? If you had searched him thoroughly you might have found evidence of his innocence—and *now* that evidence is *long gone,* isn't that correct?

---

8. *Challenge Your Sobriety at the Time You Made Relevant Observations*

Q. You testified that you just came from Mike's Restaurant when you saw my client shoot Mr. Johnson in the parking lot—correct?

Q. That's Mike's Restaurant *and Bar,* isn't it? You had some drinks, right? In fact the restaurant portion of Mike's closes at 9 p.m. and you were there until 2 a.m., isn't that correct?

Q. Smoked a little weed that night, did ya?

Q. You take Xanax, don't you? That makes you a little sleepy, doesn't it?

These are all fair and appropriate questions to ask any witness. As long as the questioner has a good faith basis for asking the question, the prosecutor will not (should not) object. Drug and alcohol use by you near the time of the event in question is fair game, because it can be relevant to show that your ability to perceive events accurately was impaired. Even questions relating to legal substances you may have consumed, if those substances could affect your perception, are proper.

YOUR TESTIMONY IS INCONSISTENT WITH THE TESTIMONY OF OTHER WITNESSES

Law enforcement witnesses should be aware that sometimes an attorney will seek to impeach you by showing you contents of a report that you did not write (This is different from the refresh your memory with anything doctrine). You cannot be impeached by a prior inconsistent statement that you did not make. It might be a proper impeachment by prior inconsistent statement if you somehow adopted (signed?) the report that was written by that other person (usually a fellow officer). An attorney cannot simply read off of somebody else's report (I have seen them do this) because the contents of that report are inconsistent with what you are saying in court now. If this is the case (*dare I say?*) the report's contents are simply hearsay.

There is nothing necessarily improper about an attorney confronting you with the fact that other people involved in the investigation perceived events differently than you perceived them. The questioner can comment, as part of his or her argument, that your testimony was different than the testimony of another. Jurors can draw whatever inferences they choose about who is telling the truth.

CHALLENGE YOUR BACKGROUND AND CREDIBILITY

What information about your personal background may an attorney use against you in his cross-examination? The law in this area is complex. It is often state and crime specific. Even so, there are some basic guidelines that you can follow wherever you are. First, never hide anything from the prosecutor that may haunt you and/or the prosecutor later. The prosecutor is like a doctor. It does you no good to lie to your doctor and no good to lie to the prosecutor. He or she will not be able to protect you from "dirt" that he or she does not know about.

More Cross Questions[146]

- What made you even notice the shooter in the first place?
- Isn't it true that the guy who robbed you was wearing a mask?
- Let me get this straight, it was dark; the lighting was poor, the guy was wearing all black—and you are sure it was my client?
- The person that you saw had a goatee and blonde hair—true? My client has black hair and he is clean shaven.
- You were drinking that entire night—isn't that so?
- Smoked a little weed that night, did you?
- You had worked a double shift so you were so tired you could barely keep your eyes open—isn't that so?
- The guy you saw was moving pretty fast—isn't that correct?
- You only saw the shooter for a couple of seconds?

— **Jack B. Swerling**
(Adapted from "Trial Advocacy")

Review Chapter Ten

- the Confrontation Clause provides that: "in all criminal prosecutions, the accused shall enjoy the right ... to be confronted with the witnesses against him"

- at its most basic level, cross-examination is simply a way of asking questions

- attorneys are permitted to ask leading questions (questions that suggest the answer; "isn't it true" questions)

- the judge presiding over the jury trial has a duty to limit cross-examination to avoid needless consumption of time

- the judge also has the duty to protect witnesses from harassment or undue embarrassment

- good cross-examiners will have you admit uncontested facts

- questions are not evidence

- cross-examiner might try to show that you are ignorant of important facts

- that you are biased

- that you have some motive to lie or exaggerate

- cross-examiner might confront you with your own allegedly inconsistent statements

- cross-examiner might try to show that your investigation could have been more thorough

- cross-examiner might try to challenge your background and credibility

Review Questions

True or False

1. Your credibility is not at issue when you are being cross-examined.
2. A defendant has a Constitutional right to confront witnesses against him.
3. The cross-examiner does not have to be nice to you.
4. The judge can permissibly limit cross-examination to only what happened on a certain day.
5. Questions are not evidence – but have fun telling attorneys that!

Multiple Choice (In the following questions, assume that the questioner has a good faith basis for asking the question.

1. *So you smoked a little weed the night of the robbery*—what is the proper response(s) when the questioner asks you to admit this on cross-examination?

   (a) Do not answer the question because it is not relevant.
   (b) Do not answer the question because it is relevant.
   (c) Tell the questioner to "Ask Snoop Dog about it" then fake a smoker's cough

   [ ] All of the above
   [ ] None of the above
   [ ] (a) and (b)

2. On cross-examination, the questioner may challenge your

   (a) credibility
   (b) eyesight
   (c) hearing

   [ ] All of the above
   [ ] None of the above
   [ ] (a) and (b)

T/F   1. F, 2. T, 3. T, 4. Not Likely, 5. T

M/C   1. None of the above, 2. All of the above, 3. All of the above, 4. (a) and (b)

3. The following question(s) are proper cross-examination questions

    (a) You are best friends with the arresting officer, isn't that correct?

    (b) You and my client were not on speaking terms for a long time—true?

    (c) The defendant owes you back child support, doesn't he?

        [   ]   All of the above
        [   ]   None of the above
        [   ]   (a) and (b)
        [   ]   (c)

4. The following question(s) are proper cross-examination questions

    (a) You wrote a report about this incident, correct? There is nothing is your report that indicates that my client "stumbled out of his car"—isn't that true?

    (b) You don't like black people, do you?

    (c) You are a homosexual, isn't that true?

        [   ]   All of the above
        [   ]   None of the above
        [   ]   (a) and (b)
        [   ]   (c)

CHAPTER ELEVEN
Preparation and Recognition

> *For my part and I hold; and Socrates made it a rule, that whoever has a vivid and clear idea in his mind will express it ...*[147]
>
> — **Montaigne**
> (From *Essays*)

Most prosecutors will help you to prepare to testify at trial and do not distinguish between general trial preparation and preparation for cross-examination. This is because, at a basic level, cross-examination is a test that the prosecution witness passes simply by knowing what she is talking about and telling the truth. Many witnesses, however, mentally prepare for cross-examination as if it were unrelated to the direct examination. This is a fiction. Cross and direct examinations are opposite sides of the same coin, for the most part. If you are prepared for one you are therefore prepared for the other. Know your stuff and tell the truth. That is all that prosecutors ask of their witnesses.

Like almost everything else in law and life, most guidelines admit exceptions. In this chapter I will focus on some challenges that await you that are unique to the experience of being cross-examined. Throughout this book I have stressed that thorough preparation is the key to effective testimony. Nothing has changed here. The best prepared witness for the prosecution is prepared generally, that is, she knows what the defense is up to in the broadest sense; and she is prepared specifically, that is, she knows how to respond to specific circumstances. In this chapter you will learn some of the most popular defenses. Become familiar with these popular defenses. They are easy to recognize. Once you identify what the defense is up to you will have a better idea of how to handle specific questions that are calculated to shade your truthful answers and make them fit into the defense's theory of the case.

Be prepared. Read every existing document that contains any statement you made about the case. If you are a police officer you must know your reports inside-out. If you are a civilian witness ask the prosecutor to permit you to review statements attributed to you in the police reports. Be prepared to discuss why the statements attributed to you in the police report might differ from the statements you might give on the witness stand presently. The defense attorney will seek to exploit even the slightest difference in what you say on the witness stand about events you witnessed and what you purportedly told police when the events were fresher in your mind. [See POPULAR WAYS TO DIS-CREDIT A WITNESS in this book.]

Because investigations of crimes often span days, months, and even years, there may be reports that are in existence that you know nothing about. Detectives often conduct follow-up inter-views of people that they reduce to writing in "Supplemental Reports." Make sure you know not only what you said and to whom, be aware of what other people said that you said. Read everything you can about the investigation, but pay special attention to statements that you made to other people about the subject matter about which you are testifying.

The defense attorney will ask you questions calculated to get you to answer consistent with his theory of the case. His theory of the case is his defense or defenses. In the next part of this chapter we will go from the general to the specific. I will address the ways defense attorneys will attack you specifically. You will learn the common ways that attorneys discredit witnesses.

RECOGNIZING THE DEFENSE THEORY OF THE CASE

Well before the famous Supreme Court decision *Gideon v. Wainwright*[148] recognized indigent defendants' the right to be represented by counsel in all felony cases, there were defense attorneys willing to work long and hard, often for little or no money, to defend the rights of the accused. However, since the 1960s, the volume of defendants represented by counsel has greatly increased. Defense attorneys, like prosecutors, do not like to reinvent the wheel. Attorneys learn tactics that have worked in the past and modify those tactics to the facts of their own case. There are few arguments used in a criminal trial that have not been used before.[149] This is good. Why? Because we can study and learn these common defenses. This way we are less likely to be surprised or caught off guard by a question or tactic.

"IF YOU CAN'T CONVINCE THEM: CONFUSE THEM"

Learn this defense because the prosecution may need your testimony to help bring clarity to the facts of the case. This is a popular defense technique in cases where there are many witnesses, or otherwise a lot of evidence. The prosecution has the burden to prove the defendant's guilt beyond a reasonable doubt.[150] Because the prosecution has the burden to prove the defendant is guilty of the crime charged, it is the defendant who benefits from any confusion. Clarity benefits the prosecution. Jurors have a duty to find a defendant guilty only when they find that the defendant committed the offense beyond a reasonable doubt.[151] Confusion creates doubt: clarity is a prerequisite of certainty.[152]

A good way to tell that a defense attorney is using this technique is if he draws a lot of objections on the basis of relevance. If the defense asks you many questions that are not relevant to the case or issue at hand, he or she may be attempting to confuse the jury. His goal may be to focus the jury's attention on many different things at once. Or he may want the jury to focus their attention on the wrong things. He may be attempting to do both. A simple example of this technique is for the defense to ask questions concerning something that the prosecution is not required to prove (also called a straw man). The prosecution does not have to prove a person's motive for committing a crime. The defendant's motive is a good piece of evidence to have, but it is not required.

Q. Isn't it true that you never saw my client arguing with [victim]?

A. Yes.

Q. Isn't it also true that you don't know if my client owned a gun?

A. I am not sure—

Q. You have no way of knowing whether he even had a valid gun license. Do you?

A. No.

The first question is an attempt to get the jury to focus on the defendant's lack of motive. The second question seeks to divert attention from "did defendant shoot victim" to whether defendant owns a gun. The third question assumes that the defendant would not shoot the victim unless the defendant possessed a valid gun license. These questions are not necessarily improper or even irrelevant. However, the cumulative effect of hundreds of these types of questions often has the effect of confusing the jury about what the law requires the prosecution to prove.

"IF YOU CAN'T CONVINCE THEM: CONFUSE THEM" VS. "THE SPAGHETTI DEFENSE"

Many people confuse "If You Can't Convince ..." with the "Spaghetti Defense." This is because these defenses belong to the family of defenses that seeks to benefit from jury confusion. I will discuss the "Spaghetti Defense" next. Both defenses, when they work, work because they sufficiently distract the jury from the real facts or issues of the case. The "If You Can't Convince ..." defense distracts the jury by directing their attention to "so what" (aka: irrelevant) facts. For example: The defendant could be a "nice guy" *and* the defendant could have committed this murder. Those two things can be true at the same time. The truth or falsity of the defendant's "niceness" has very little, if anything, to do with whether he did or did not commit the crime charged. The defense attorney hopes that the jury will be wrapped up considering so many irrelevant details that they will lose sight of the facts and issues that are important. The "Spaghetti Defense," like its cousin, "If You Can't Convince ...," employs a strategy that is designed to confuse the jury. However, the "Spaghetti Defense," confuses by posing multiple, often contradictory defenses (e.g., self-defense, alibi, etc.) at the same time. Each defense, con-sidered by itself, is likely to be coherent and relevant to the facts of the case. However, they cannot all be true at the same time. The defense attorney simply hopes that one juror will buy one of the defenses. Therefore, this strategy can work and often does work because of and not in spite of its overall incoherence.

The "Spaghetti Defense" is a very popular all-purpose defense. This defense is characterized by a defense that throws everything at the wall to see what sticks. If you throw a bowl of spaghetti at the wall something is bound to stick (unless you enjoy your spaghetti super al dente. The Spaghetti Defense generally focuses on the law rather than the facts. The Spaghetti Defense can be a very effective tool in the hands of an experienced defense attorney.

"Spaghetti Defense"	"If You Can't Convince Them: Confuse Them"
My client is not guilty because he:	My client is not guilty because he:
1. didn't do it 2. it was self-defense 3. he wasn't even there 4 he was protecting his wife 5. he is insane	1. is not that kind of guy 2. loves the victim 3. hates guns 4. is a member of the clergy 5. is a nice guy 6. it happened on a Tuesday

It is important for witnesses to learn to identify these defenses because the prosecution may need your testimony to help focus the jury's attention on the relevant issues. The Spaghetti Defense argument is generally coherent and easy to follow. However, the claims made by the defense attorney are mutually incompatible. How can it be both "self-defense" and "the defendant wasn't there" at the same time? It can't. Consistency among arguments does not matter, what matters is that at least one juror buys at least one of the arguments. If one juror buys one argument, at minimum, the defendant receives the benefit of a hung jury.

The If You Can't Convince ... defense, on the other hand, is generally incoherent and hard to follow. The defense attorney hopes by presenting the jury with a confusing jumble of mostly irrelevant facts that the jury will simply throw up its collective hands in frustration and conclude that they don't know what happened; or, the truth can never be known. Either way a confused jury is unlikely to find a defendant guilty beyond a reasonable doubt.

"POLICE FRAME-UP DEFENSE" AKA "O.J. DEFENSE"

Learn this defense because the prosecution may need your testimony to rebut a claim of police frame-up. Before Johnnie Cochran made the "Police Frame-Up Defense" popular in the trial of O. J. Simpson (*now a convicted felon*), defense attorneys had been using this defense, with mixed success, for as long as there had been police and defendants. This defense fades in and out of popularity. It is probably the least effective of the many defenses available in a defense attorney's tool kit. This defense, if it works at all, usually works only in the most serious of cases. This is because a police frame-up argument is vulnerable to the following prosecution argument:

> "If the police were trying to frame this defendant, as the defense implied with her argument, why stop at [burglary], [possession of controlled substance], [retail theft], etc. ... why not toss a kilo of cocaine in his trunk, or maybe a dead prostitute?"

Note: This prosecution retort doesn't work if the defendant is in fact charged with possession of a kilo of cocaine or killing a prostitute. The Police Frame-Up Defense is hard to sell to juries because people tend to believe that *most* police are honest most of the time. Even in communities where police/citizen relations are not what they should be, the Police Frame-Up Defense is not likely to work. There is simply little benefit to the police. I imagine that the time and effort it would take to frame an innocent person (yes, the guilty can be framed too) would not be worth the trouble. Why would a police officer risk his or her career to frame a "nobody" for a relatively minor felony? It defies common sense. This however, leads to a better, more successful defense.

"EVERYBODY IS INCOMPETENT DEFENSE" AKA "HINDSIGHT DEFENSE"

Learn this defense because the prosecution may need your testimony to present what investigators did right and what doesn't matter. This defense is often successful because it is largely true. All humans, no matter how skilled, are going to make mistakes. There will never be a case where *every* participant, or *any* participant for that matter, performs his or her duties perfectly. Be prepared to answer questions about what you could have done but didn't do, and questions about what you did do but shouldn't have done. This defense is the most popular of the "raise the burden of proof" defenses. Good defense attorneys are expert in taking a case apart piece by piece, with the benefit of hindsight, to show every mistake no matter how small *or insignificant*, with the goal of convincing the jury that they can never, in good conscience, find the defendant guilty based on the evidence derived from such a flawed investigation. This defense is often very effective. It is possibly the most effective defense because it is very easy to find mistakes in every investigation.[153]

"SOG"

(Some Other Guy Did it Defense)

You can easily identify this defense because the defense attorney will spend a great deal of time cross-examining witnesses regarding identification defects in the prosecution's case.[154] For instance, the witness was too far away to see the defendant accurately. It was too dark. The witness was drunk or high (aka "Snoop Dog Defense"). It happened too fast. The witness was concentrating on the gun and not the defendant. The witness was distracted. The defendant's face was covered. When police arrested the defendant he was wearing a black shirt and the witness told police that the gunman was wearing a brown shirt. The police identification procedure was too suggestive.[155] Identification defects come in an almost infinite variety. What they have in common is that these defenses highlight the inherent uncertainty and fallibility of human perception. When done well, this is a good defense because nobody wants to convict the wrong person.

"DNA DEFENSE"
(aka "CSI Defense": Prosecutor's "DNA" = "Does Not Apply")

"Ladies and gentlemen of the jury; I ask you—where's the DNA? Where's the fingerprints? Why didn't they do spectral analysis?"[156] Sure, the defendant is accused of committing a retail theft, but that's no excuse for the police not to do accident reconstruction just to be safe! What about the defendant's hemoglobin? Didn't anybody think to check that?" The "DNA Defense" does not have to necessarily involve the prosecution's use or non-use of DNA. Defense attorneys use this defense every time they argue to the jury that the only way they can find the defendant guilty is if the state produced _____ (fill in the blank) evidence. The state did not produce _____ (fill in the blank) evidence; therefore, the defendant is not guilty. In the field of logic the DNA Defense is also known as a "straw man argument." Neither the defense attorney nor the attorney for the prosecution get to decide, in advance, what type of evidence the jury members need as a prerequisite to determine the defendant's guilt. This decision is entirely up to the members of the jury. When a judge rules that the jurors can consider X and/or Y in their deliberations, then they can consider X and/or Y to determine defendant's guilt. It is for the jury to decide if, in addition to X and Y they need Z to find the defendant guilty. Judges are not always perfect. Judges often let juries consider improper evidence and keep out evidence that is proper. The fallibility of judges has little to do with the DNA Defense because this defense is always about what evidence the prosecution did not present to the jury. It is more about quantity and type of evidence than it is about the quality of the evidence presented to the jury.

An effective DNA Defense accomplishes one or both of the following. Effective use of the DNA Defense may cause the jury to misunderstand the prosecution's burden of proof. The prosecution has to prove that the defendant is guilty of the offense or offenses beyond a *reasonable* doubt—not beyond all doubt.[157] Second, effective use of the DNA Defense may cause the jury to misunderstand the relationship between the quantity of evidence and the certainty of a defendant's guilt.[158]

Is it legally permissible for a jury to find a defendant guilty without the prosecution presenting any of the following: DNA, fingerprints, video surveillance, handwriting comparisons, and chemical composition analysis of fibers, etc.? Yes.[159] The prosecution's burden of proof does not increase every time there is a scientific advancement. It remains the same. The prosecution's burden of proof is "beyond a reasonable doubt."

The Defense May Ask You Questions That Are Calculated to Show:

- Your account of the incident makes no sense or is illogical based on other known facts.
- Your perception of the incident was inadequate.
- Your objectivity is questionable because you are biased or have some interest in the outcome of the prosecution's case.
- You made some prior statements, either orally or in writing, that are inconsistent with what you are saying now.[160]

THE UNCROSS-EXAMINED LIFE IS WORTH LIVING

Not every witness gets cross-examined. There are many strategic reasons why a good attorney might choose not to cross-examine a witness; or only ask witness one or two questions on cross-examination and then sit down. If the witness does not hurt your case, or if the witness helps your case, it is often good strategy to ask nothing. Also, as I touched on earlier in this chapter, many attorneys do not like to *harshly* cross-examine sympathetic witnesses like the elderly or children. Knowing this you should still expect that the defense attorney will cross-examine you. He or she will almost certainly ask you questions that concern at least one if not all of the following topics.

1. Opportunity to Observe   2. Ability to Perceive
3. Accuracy of Description

TWO SPECIAL TYPES OF WITNESS

The Dolphin

"The Dolphin" is a species of witness that is irredeemable. He's a flipper and everybody knows that he's a flipper. What is a flipper? A flipper is a person who completely and totally changes his story on the witness stand. Changes from what? He changes everything about the substance of what he originally said to either the police or the prosecution or both. This is a person who no longer wants to testify and/or thinks it's a good idea to commit perjury because he has changed his mind. The Dolphin witness is different from the "Jellyfish" or "Guppy Witness." The Dolphin, like the Jellyfish and Guppy, does not want to testify. However, unlike the Jellyfish and Guppy, the Dolphin wants to actively hurt the prosecution's case. Dolphins are often members of street gangs. Dolphins are often the victims of the very crime about which they are now perjuring themselves. Dolphins are generally bad people. In almost all cases there will be minor inconsistencies between what you said at an earlier time and what you say on the witness stand. This is inevitable. Memories degrade; minds sometimes fill in parts of stories to make memories consistent narratives of events. These may be very minor details. You are not lying because you actually remember things slightly differently as the time between the event and your testimony grows longer.

The best sign that you are being treated like a Dolphin is when the defense attorney challenges literally everything you say. The defense attorney will point to every possible inconsistency no matter how trivial. The best way to handle being treated like a Dolphin is for you to admit when you are not sure about something; if true, "I don't know" is a completely acceptable answer to any question. Other than that, the best way to effectively testify when the defense attorney is treating you like a Dolphin is to let it happen. Do not react at all. Do not scowl or roll your eyes or argue with the defense attorney. If you are not really a Dolphin the jury will figure this out after listening to you answer a few questions. The defense attorney will slowly, but ever so surely, question-by-trivial-question, begin to sound like a bully and a jerk. Jury's do not like bullies. Nobody likes jerks.

Never interfere with a defense attorney when she is in the process of eroding her own credibility.

Q. And when he was placed under arrest, he was placed in a small room, is that correct?

A. He was placed in an interview room in Area 2.

Q. And typically, that is called a box?

A. I don't think I have ever heard it called that, but—

[Take a second to think about your answer. If you have been a detective for 30 years, 12 years in Area 2, and you never heard anyone refer to the interview room as a "box" then the truthful answer is no. This is also an example of an (unethical?) tactic when an attorney attempts to suggest a piece of evidence he or she never intends to introduce (prove-up) for the purpose of placing it into the minds of jurors.]

THE DODDER-HEAD AKA "PRECARIOUS-PETE" OR "SHAKY-SALLY"

The "Dodder-head" is a goof. He or she *might* be a pathological liar; but is *likely* to be just a lonely person who likes receiving attention. Unlike the Dolphin, the Dodder-head has no real reason or motive to lie. At least no reason that anybody can think of. The Dodder-head is cool one moment and shaky the next. Dodder-heads can be either a defense or a prosecution witness. However, they are almost always beneficial to the defense because their testimony fits so well with the ever-popular "If You Can't Convince Them: Confuse Them" defense. Neither the defense nor the prosecution has motivation to *knowingly* put a Dodder-head on the witness stand. Even though Dodder-heads usually benefit the defense, they are too unpredictable be used reliably. Also, the vast majority of defense attorneys will not call a witness that he or she knows is going to commit perjury.

TIPS FOR TESTIFYING ON CROSS-EXAMINATION

Maintain eye contact with attorney asking the question,
the judge, and the jury

Sitting in a witness stand is not natural. However, try to be
as natural as possible under the circumstances. That means you
first must look at the person who is asking the questions. If you
were having a conversation with someone at a party or in a
supermarket, you would maintain eye contact with the person
you were talking to. Now imagine a crowd gathering. They are
interested in your conversation. You might look at them periodi-
cally. They are the judge and jury. There is no correct answer as
to how much eye contact to maintain with the person questioning
you versus the judge and jury; there are, however, incorrect
answers. Do not look at your feet. Do not stare off into the
distance. If you are being cross-examined, never look to the
prosecutor (help me!) if you are confused or stuck on a question.

Listen to the Question and
Answer Only the Question Asked

Ambiguous Question[161]
Is subject to two or more interpretations.

Vague Question[162]
Is a question that has an uncertain meaning.

This guideline seems obvious, but it's not as easy to do in
practice. There are several ways that even the best listeners can
have problems with this guideline. Sometimes an attorney will
ask a question that is unclear or imprecise. On these occasions it
is entirely appropriate for you to ask for clarification. Do not
answer a question that you truly do not understand. This helps
nobody. Never use feigned confusion to avoid answering a hard
question on cross-examination. This makes you look evasive and
untrustworthy. It is not the witness's job to confront facts that are
contrary to the prosecution's case. Your job is to tell the truth in
the clearest and most understandable way possible. Prosecutors
make arguments. You make facts. Try not to anticipate what the

questioner actually means. If the question is straightforward, answer it in a straightforward way.

EXAMPLES

Q. How far were you from the train station when you say that you saw the guy who you say was, my client, and the guy who you say robbed the convenience store?
A. *I do not understand your question.* (GOOD ANSWER)

[Defendant was identified getting into the passenger's side of a *blue truck* immediately after robbing the convenience[163] store.]

Q. Isn't it true that when you arrested my client he was driving a *red* car?
A. Your client switched cars after the robbery; he switched out of the blue truck—but that doesn't mean ...

(Do not give an explanation. This is a simple question. Give a simple answer.) (Note, however: You do not always have to give a "yes or no" answer to a "yes or no" question; however, when asked a straight-forward question, you should give a straight-forward answer.)

Q. Isn't it true that when you pulled my client over, he wasn't doing anything illegal?
A. Well, first of all ...
Q. Yes or no!

This question, at best, is imprecise. It is impossible to correctly (truthfully) answer an imprecise question without guessing what the questioner is referring to. What if, for example, you pulled his client over on more than one occasion? To which occasion is the defense attorney referring? The problem with a question like this one is that the question lacks foundation. Foundation is the "when," where," and "with whom" information that you need to give a straightforward answer. Never answer a question that you do not understand. The prosecutor will often object to imprecise questions. If the judge sustains the prosecutor's objection, the defense attorney will be required to rephrase his question. Therefore, you will not have to answer the question. If the prosecutor fails to object, simply answer by saying that you do not understand the question or if the question could be fairly interpreted as referring to any one of two or more occasions, it is permissible for you to indicate to the judge that the question is ambiguous. Inquire into which occasion the questioner seeks comment. If you find it necessary to obtain clarification before answering a question, direct any inquiries to the judge, not the questioner. "Judge, I do not understand the question." Not: "Listen bone-head, I'm not a mind reader, I bet we could move things along if at least some of your questions made some sense some of the time. Members of the jury, is it me, or is this guy an idiot?"

[The shooting happened October, 10, *2011*.]

Q. You said that the night Bobby shot you, October, 10, *2010*, it was cold. True?

A. No

(The defense attorney made a mistake. He got the date wrong. Use this opportunity to show that you are fair. Resist the urge to shove it in his face. Be nice even if he is not. Do not play word games. This is one of the rare instances where you should break the "answer only the question asked" rule. As a general rule you should not attempt to figure out what the opposing attorney means. You should only answer his question. However, when he or she clearly made a mistake, it is perfectly acceptable (advisable) to be nice about it. It is okay for you to answer the above question in the following way:

A. You mean *2011*. Yes. Yes it was cold that night.

(Give a response like this one rather than a snarky response.)

Pace Your Answers

It is imperative that you permit enough time for the prosecutor to object to defense attorney's question. However, if you think that a question is improper do not turn and look at the prosecutor as if to say, *aren't you going to object*. There are many strategic reasons why a prosecutor might not object to an objectionable question. Moreover, many prosecutors do not like to interrupt the flow of testimony for minor evidentiary violations. This is especially true when the answer to the question is helpful to the prosecution's case. On cross-examination your questioner will invariably try to establish a rhythm. Disturb that rhythm by changing speed and using pauses.[164]

- Answer questions at your own pace.
- Think before you speak.
- Don't permit the defense attorney to rush your answer.
- Speak at your *natural rate*.
- Speak at an *unnaturally loud* volume. (If you normally speak softly.)

Do Not Volunteer Information

This guideline is true no matter who is asking you the question. If the prosecution wants additional information from you she will ask. Offering volunteered information to the defense may at best be a waste of time, thus annoying to the jury; at worst, your additional information may be improper, subject the prosecutor to sanction, or even be cause for a mistrial. In any case volunteering information violates the guideline I discussed above, listen to the question and answers only the question asked.

When you offer additional information than the question asked for, in addition to the above reasons, you give more words that an unscrupulous defense attorney might later use against you. What harm is there in volunteering information to the prosecution that is favorable to the prosecution? See the following example.

EXAMPLES

[The witness in the following example is being asked questions by the prosecution on direct examination. Prosecution witnesses often perceive direct examination as the "easy part." This perception is mostly correct. The prosecutor will be asking the questions and you are a prosecution witness. Also, you presumably have

prepared your testimony in advance (but not your exact answers!). No surprises here.]

Q. Do you see in court the person who took your wallet?
A. Yes. (Good so far.)
Q. Please point to and identify and article of clothing that this
person is wearing.
A. Yes. He is the guy in the Orange DOC jumpsuit with the
Latin Kings gang tattoo on his right arm that is covered up by
some sort of large gauze band-aid.

This answer is 22, words too long (21 if "band-aid" is one word)!
A seemingly innocuous answer such as this can in some cases
cause a mistrial. Why? There may have been a previous order by
the judge that prohibited any person from commenting on the
defendant's gang affiliation. Something like this could be cause
for a mistrial.

Never Guess

If you do not know, say so. Again, never use feigned ignorance
to avoid answering a hard question on cross-examination. You
may get away with this once or twice. But it makes you look
dishonest, and it is dishonest. If true, however, "I don't know" is
a perfectly acceptable answer.

EXAMPLES

Q. From the time the vehicle was stopped to the time that Mr.
Reeves was taken from the scene by the police, how many
minutes elapsed?
A. *I don't recall how many minutes.*[165]

Avoid

EXACTERATIONS[166]

"pretending to be *completely sure* about a
proposition, premise or argument that, about
which, you could not possibly have a clue"

Do Not Argue

Often inexperienced attorneys think that yelling and screaming at a witness is equivalent to effective cross-examination of that witness. It is not. However, there are occasions where a good attorney will attempt to rattle you, by raising his or her voice, tricking you, or engaging in any number of techniques calculated to discredit you. If you feel like this is happening to you, your best response is to immediately and subtly do the exact opposite. If the questioner is yelling at you, gradually lower your voice. If he is being rude, you be polite. If he is speaking fast in order to confuse you, you speak slower. Be like Plumper the house cat. At rest on the window sill, *yawning* as Rocky the German Shepard barks violently right below the window, Plumper simply licks her paws and falls back asleep. Drives them crazy every time.

Even though it is never a good idea to argue with your questioner, it is permissible to *gently* correct the questioner to avoid misstatements of fact.[167]

EXAMPLE

Q. At the time you made a *left-hand* turn onto Golf Road, you had no idea who was in that car?

A. I turned *right* on Golf Road, yes. (Emphasis added.)

Do Not Permit Questioner to Bully You

If you are sure about your answer then do not change that answer. Stay firm and do not equivocate. If the answer you gave is the truth—stick with it. Do not permit the questioner to bully you into giving a different answer or changing the words of your answer to his or her liking. You provide the testimony and the questioner asks the questions. If he or she is unsatisfied with your answer to a question—that's too bad! This does not mean that you should ignore what you just read in the previous example. Of course you should not argue with the questioner. Simply stay firm. Remain composed. Stick with your answer.

Make sure you familiarize yourself with everything you said about this case to before your present testimony. If you testified before at another hearing make sure you read those transcripts. If you gave statements to police read those reports. If you are an officer or investigator, at minimum, you must read all of *your* reports. Be prepared to explain any differences in your present testimony and any statements you made in the past. There are many legitimate reasons why one's testimony might change slightly over time. Make sure you are prepared to explain those reasons.[168]

EXAMPLE[169]

Do not make deals with the questioner other than to tell the whole truth. Often, cross-examiners will ask you to commit to answering his "yes or no" questions with a "yes or no" response. Politely decline this trap. If a yes or no response, in the context of the question, is the truth, you will answer the question "yes or no," otherwise your responsibility is to tell the truth.[170]

Never Deny that You Spoke About the Case with the Prosecutor

Because this answer is not true and everybody knows it! You must tell the truth. There is nothing wrong with preparing for court testimony. There is nothing wrong with talking with the prosecutor before giving testimony. As long as the prosecutor does not tell you to lie you have nothing to worry about. The prosecutor should prepare you to testify. He or she will not have you rehearse your testimony. Rehearsed testimony comes across flat and insincere; and therefore, it is no benefit to the prosecution.

Stop Talking Immediately When there Is an Objection

If either the prosecution or the defense objects to *anything* stop talking and wait for the judge to rule upon the attorney's objection.

Conclusion

Relax, be yourself, tell the truth, and you'll do just fine.

Review Chapter Eleven

- most prosecutors will help you to prepare to testify at trial and do not distinguish between general trial preparation and preparation for cross-examination

- the prosecution will only expect two things from you, know your stuff, and tell the truth

- read every document that exists that contains any statement that you made about the case

- preparation is the key to effective testimony

- never attempt to memorize your testimony

- defense benefits from jury confusion

- when defense employs the "if you can't convince them: confuse them" defense, he is seeking to benefit from jury confusion

- "spaghetti defense," confuses the jury by posing multiple, often contradictory defenses

- "police frame-up defense," if it works at all, generally only works when defendant is charged with a very serious crime

- good defense attorneys are expert in taking a case apart piece by piece, with the benefit of hindsight, to show every mistake you made no matter how small or insignificant

- dolphins are liars

- dodder-heads are goofs

- jellyfish and guppies are cowards

Review Questions

True or False

1. Proper preparation does not mean memorization.
2. Dolphins swim against the current (if "with the current" means "tell the truth").
3. Prosecutors prefer a good confused jury. They are easier to manipulate.
4. Do not roll your eyes if the defense attorney asks you a stupid question.
5. "Precarious-Pete" is probably a pretty lonely person.

Multiple-Choice

1. If the defense attorney, in his closing argument, seems confused as to why the prosecution did not call an expert witness to testify about soil erosion, in a case involving a forged check, he is likely attempting to use the _____ defense.

   (a) DNA
   (b) SOG
   (c) Hindsight

   [ ]   All of the above
   [ ]   None of the above
   [ ]   (a)
   [ ]   (b) and (c)

2. Chances are the defense attorney will question you concerning your

   (a) opportunity to observe
   (b) ability to perceive accurately
   (c) accuracy of description

   [ ]   All of the above
   [ ]   None of the above
   [ ]   (a) and (b)
   [ ]   (a)

3. "Jellyfish" witnesses are wimps, rascally rude-hearted wimps, however, they are

   (a) not usually out to get anybody
   (b) not likely to show up to court to screw-up the prosecution's case anyway
   (c) unlike "Dolphins"

   [　]　All of the above
   [　]　None of the above
   [　]　(a)
   [　]　(a) and (c)

ENDNOTES

[1] Not all mistakes are opportunities for personal growth. Some mistakes are career-enders. What is the difference between the two types of mistakes? I'm not really sure. I guess the only true way to know whether you have made a career ending mistake is when two sour-faced security guards "escort" you out of your place of business. My point is this: Nietzsche was quite wrong when he wrote "That which does not kill me makes me stronger." Some things that don't kill you *actually make you much weaker*. Repeatedly making the same mistake over and over for example. If that doesn't immediately kill your career it certainly contributes to its slow painful demise.

[2] See above.

[3] I use the word "confirmed" loosely. Effective court communication is part art and part science. An idea or technique is "confirmed" to the extent that I included it in this book means that it meets the four criteria I write about in the following paragraph.

[4] There must be some confirmation in the writings of historical experts in oratory, persuasion, or related topic. Experts such as Aristotle, Cicero, and Shakespeare, for example, did not always agree on the matters found in this book; however, when they did agree they were surprisingly uniform of opinion.

[5] Included in my analysis were "observations" I made of witnesses' live testimony contained within the thousands of pages of criminal court transcripts.

[6] Ekman, Paul, "A Few Can Catch A Liar." *Psychological Science,* VOL. 10(3) (1999).

[7] Homer, *The Odyssey*, p. 395, Lines 166–169, Translated by Robert Fagles, Penguin Classics Deluxe Edition (1997).

[8] Apple, William; Streeter, Lynn; Krauss, Robert, *Journal of Personality and Social Psychology*, 715–727, Vol. 37 (May 1979) "Speakers with high-pitched voices were judged less truthful, less emphatic, less 'potent' ... and more nervous. Slow-talking speakers were judged less truthful, less fluent, and less persuasive ..."

[9] "Many trial attributes have theatrical qualities: the stylized and ritualistic dialogue ('May it please the court'; 'If your honor please'); the fact that the attorneys serve as intermediaries between the judge and the (mostly silent) defendants; the public rising when the jury enters and leaves; the movement created by the jury obediently entering and leaving the courtroom at the judge's command ..." Lahav, Pnina, Theater In The Courtroom: The Chicago Conspiracy Trial , 16 Law & Literature 381, 391–392 (Fall, 2004).

[10] *Rosenblum, Steven, People v. Chambers*, at 32. (From unpublished transcript.)

[11] Parties are prohibited from presenting arguments in their opening statement. The purpose of opening statement it to acquaint the judge or jury with the facts you expect to show at trial. Notwithstanding this prohibition, most attorneys (knowingly or unknowingly) slip arguments into their opening statement.

[12] Aristotle maintained that people take into account the moral character of the speaker as much as they do the content of their speech. "[Persuasion is affected] by means of moral character, when the speech shall have been spoken in such a way as to render the speaker *worthy of confidence ...*" *Aristotle's Treatise on Rhetoric*, Book I, p. 12, translated by Theodore Buckley (George Bell & Sons, London, New York 1894).

[13] See Gershman, Bennett, "The Prosecutor's Duty to Truth," 14 Geo. J. Legal Ethics 309 (Winter 2001).

[14] See Gershman, Bennett, "The Prosecutor's Duty to Truth," 14 Geo. J. Legal Ethics 309 (Winter 2001).

[15] Quoting Aristotle, United States Supreme Court Justice Antonin Scalia and co-author Bryan A. Garner write "We believe good men more fully and more readily than others ..." Antonin Scalia and Bryan A. Garner, *Making Your Case: Art of Persuading Judges*, p. XXIII, Thompson/West Publishers (2008); Judge Ferrill D. McRae, at the opening of Alabama courts, aptly quoted Edward R. Morrow "To be persuasive, we must be believable. To be believable, we must be credible. To be credible, we must be truthful." *58 Ala. Law 37*, 38 (1997).

[16] "We think of testimony as working in much more direct ways [than other ways to communicate such as parable], as when you want to tell me it's raining outside, and say 'It's raining.' In normal cases ... speakers who want to communicate something to us do so using words and sentences that actually mean what they want to communicate." Currie, Gregory, "Telling Stories," p.46, from *The Philosophers' Magazine Issue 54* (3rd Quarter 2011).

[17] Kelly, Lynn & Keaton, James, "Treating Communication Anxiety: Implications of the Communibiological Paradigm," *Communication Education*, p.45, Vol.49, No.1, "For the majority of Americans ... public speaking is the most feared communication context" (January, 2000).

[18] See Kelly & Keaton "Treating Communication Anxiety ..." pp. 45–57.

[19] Montaigne (quoting Horace), *The Complete Essays Of Montaigne*, p.125, Translated by Donald M. Frame, Stanford University Press (2007).

[20] Galves, Fred, Where the Not-So-Wild Things Are: Computers in the Courtroom, the Federal Rules of Evidence, and the Need for Institutional Reform and More Judicial Acceptance, *13 Harv. J. Law & Tec 161*, 186 (Winter 2000).

[21] Montaigne (quoting Seneca), *The Complete Essays Of Montaigne*, p.127, translated by Donald M. Frame, Stanford University Press (2007).

[22] United States Constitution Amendment VI "In all criminal prosecutions, the accused shall enjoy the right to a speedy and public trial, by an impartial jury of the State and district wherein the crime shall have been committed ..." See also, Article III (Sec. 2). The United States Constitution; The United States Supreme Court restated and expanded the conception of the right to a jury trial in the year 2000. The Court made it clear that the right to a trial by jury even applies to the *sentencing phase of trial* under certain circumstances. *Apprendi v. New Jersey*, 530 U.S. 466,476–478 (2000) (Internal citations omitted).

[23] *Apprendi* at 477.

[24] Rachlinski, Jeffery, Symposium: Empirical Legal Realism: A New Social Scientific Assessment of Law and Human Behavior: The Uncertain Psychological Case for Paternalism, *97 Nw. UL. Rev. 1165*, 1168 (Spring 2003); see also Sunstein, Cass (ed.), *Behavioral Law and Economics*, Cambridge University Press, (2000).

[25] *Sullivan v. Louisiana*, 508 U.S. 275, 278 (1993); see *Patterson v. New York*, 432 U.S. 197, 210 (1977), "The Due Process Clause requires the prosecution to prove beyond a reasonable doubt all of the elements included in the definition of the offense of which the defendant is charged."

[26] There may be one of many strategic reasons why a prosecutor might split the duties differently. This is a case-specific decision.

[27] This is also the part of the prosecution's argument that gets the prosecutor in the most trouble. It is very tempting for a prosecutor to overstep his bounds and say something improper in rebuttal. When cases are reversed or otherwise criticized by appellate courts based on improper prosecutorial comments, these comments were more often than not made in rebuttal.

[28] Sunstein, Cass (ed.), *Behavioral Law and Economics*, Cambridge University Press, (2000).

[29] A "motion" is simply a way to ask the judge to rule on a specific request.

[30] Because criminal law is state specific (subject to the federal Constitution), the order and substance of motions differ from jurisdiction to jurisdiction. Every court, however, has the motions discussed here. They are called by different names, but in substance most of these motions are the same.

[31] Richard McKeon, *Introduction to Aristotle*, 336 (The Modern Library ed. Random House 1947) (Quoting Aristotle, Nicomachean Ethics BK. II Ch. 3). (Aristotle presages Forrest Gump, "stupid is as stupid does.")

[32] There is an exception to the "personal knowledge" requirement for expert witnesses.

[33] Jokes by Steven Wright, Downloaded August 26, 2011, at 12:54 pm. from *http://www.wright-house.com/steven-wright/steven-wright-As.html*.

[34] *The Social Psychology of Good and Evil* (ed.) Arthur G. Miller, p.304, DePaulo, Bella, *The Many Faces of Lies*, The Guilford Press (2005).

[35] *Berger v. United States*, 295 U.S. 78, 88 (1935). (This case addressed the ethical obligations of United States Attorneys; however, the Court's logic applies equally to state and local prosecutors.)

[36] *United States v. Ash*, 413 U.S. 300, 320 (1973), citing *Berger v. United States*, 295 U.S. 78, 88 (1935); Brady v. Maryland, 373 U.S. 83, 87–88 (1963).

[37] *Deutch v. United States*, 367 US 456 (1961).

[38] *Brady v. Maryland*, 373, U.S. 83 (1963).

[39] *People of State of Illinois v. Turner Reeves*, Unpublished Transcript, pp. 11–12, NO. 02CF 1617 (March 2005).

[40] Generally the prosecutor conducts the direct examination of the police officer. However, there are some defense motions that require the defendant to put on his evidence first. Under these circumstances it is the defense attorney who conducts the direct examination. Here he is attempting to get the police officer to admit that the defendant did not commit any crimes and had no active warrants for his arrest. Therefore, the police conducted an illegal stop of the defendant's car.

[41] *People v. Reeves* at 12.

[42] It is probably a good idea to be polite and courteous to people anyway.

43 If, however, you are actually an obnoxious, loud and rude person, then by all means do not be yourself!

44 Carroll, Lewis and Introduction by Martin Gardner, *The Annotated Alice: The Definitive Edition*, p. 313, W.W. Norton & Company, NY (2000).

45 Throughout this book I often cite The Federal Rules of Evidence. I use the FRE as a common point of reference. They will not necessarily apply in the jurisdiction where you will be testifying. However, most jurisdictions, if they have not adopted the Federal Rules outright, have *similar* rules of evidence. As always, it is important to check the local and state rules that govern your particular jurisdiction.

46 They won't put you into the strait-jacket until after they admit you into the "institution."

47 FRE R. 611 (a)

48 Pinker, Steven, *the blank slate* (small case letters in original), *The Modern Denial of Human Nature*, p. 259, Penguin Books Publishing (2002).

49 *Social Psychology*, 2nd Edition (Aronson, E., Wilson, T., Akert, R.). Addison-Wesley Educational Publishers, Inc. New York (1997); see also, *Yale Attitude Change Approach*; Yale University Study (Hovland, Janis, & Kelley, 1953). (The "Yale Attitude Change Approach" mirrors Aristotle: "The effectiveness of persuasive communications depends on who says what to whom." Who: Credible experienced etc. What: People are more persuaded by messages that do not seem to be designed to influence them. *Social Psychology* at 237.)

50 Sunstein, Cass (Ed.), *Behavioral Law & Economics*, Cambridge University Press (2007).

51 Aristotle, *Rhetoric*, Dover Thrift Edition, p.5 (Originally published Oxford University Press, 1924, 2004).

52 Aristotle, *Rhetoric*, Dover Thrift Edition (Originally published Oxford University Press, 1924, 2004).

53 Apple, William; Streeter, Lynn; Krauss, Robert, *Journal of Personality and Social Psychology*, 715–727, Vol. 37 (May 1979).

54 Levenson, Laurie, *"Courtroom Demeanor: The Theater of the Courtroom,"* 92 Mi. L. Rev. 573, 574 (2008).

55 Wisotsky, Steven, "Sounds and Images of Persuasion: A Primer," *84 Fla. Bar J.* 40, 1–2 (2010) Quoting Aristotle's *Rhetoric*.

[56] You should note that I did *not* write "The best *rehearsed* witnesses are the most effective witnesses." Do not confuse preparation with *rehearsed memorization*. Even if it were possible to memorize your testimony, it would be a bad idea to do so. You do not want to appear to be reading from a script. This sort of testimony makes you appear dishonest and it is also an ineffective way to communicate in an inherently dynamic setting like a courtroom.

[57] Aristotle, *Rhetoric*, P. V, Dover Thrift Edition (Originally published Oxford University Press, 1924, 2004).

[58] Aristotle's used of the Greek "Pathos" referred to the speaker's appeal to his audience's emotions when attempting to persuade them. It is generally impermissible for a prosecutor to *directly appeal* to the judge's or jury's emotions when making arguments. Notwithstanding this prohibition, there will almost always be an emotional content to a criminal trial. Prosecutors' are not prohibited from addressing emotionally charged issues. Most courts permit prosecutor's to address emotional elements of a case as long as he does not make the "appeal to emotion or sympathy" the basis (or even a large part) of his argument. This is a difficult legal controversy and beyond the scope of this book.

[59] Stephanie A. Vaughan, "Persuasion Is An Art ... But It Is Also an Invaluable Tool in Advocacy," *61 Baylor L. Rev. 635*, 680–683 (2009).

[60] See Sunstein, *Law and Economics* (2000).

[61] See Sunstein, *Law and Economics* (2000).

[62] Aristotle, *Rhetoric* at V.

[63] Milton, John, *Paradise Lost*, p.110: lines 114–117, Barnes & Noble Classics, NY (based on 2nd Ed. 1674; 2004). (In Milton's famous Epic Poem *Paradise Lost*, Satan changed his demeanor and physical appearance so that he could trespass into the Garden of Eden without arising suspicion. Satan's trick worked—initially. Satan fooled the Archangel Uriel, who was guarding the newly created world. Satan accomplished his trickery by changing his appearance and turning himself into a youthful and graceful "stripling cherub ... [baby faced angel]." Lines 636–639; However, Satan's ruse was short-lived as he soon learned that it is difficult for one to *fake* one's demeanor for long. Eventually your true demeanor will shine-through. Uriel observed Satan, who was, by then, standing on the far away Mount Niphates, "his gestures [were] fierce... and [his] demeanor [mad]...." Lines 128–129. Satan's physical movements, that is, his demeanor, ultimately betrayed his true character. The lesson from this small part of Paradise Lost is that demeanor matters: but so does sincerity. You can and should conduct yourself a way that is open and friendly. You

can and should strive to use the techniques of the experts whom I quote in this book. That said: seek to improve your demeanor within the range of your *true personality*—be yourself. Unless, of course, you are Milton's Satan. If this is the case; don't be yourself.

[64] Hon. Timony, James, Demeanor Credibility, *49 Cath. U.L. Rev. 903*, p. 912 (2000).

[65] The following is a "typical" jury instruction: Illinois Pattern Jury Instruction 1.02: JURY IS THE SOLE JUDGE OF THE BELIEVA-BILITY OF WITNESSES; "Only you are the judges of the believability of the witnesses and of the weight to be given to the testimony of each one of them. In considering the testimony of any witness, you may take into account his ability and opportunity to observe, his memory, his manner while testifying, *any interest, bias, or prejudice he may have*, and the reasonableness of his testimony considered in the light of all the evidence in the case." IPI 1.02. (Emphasis added.)

[66] The fact that most jury instructions warn jurors to consider a witness's possible bias or prejudice, along with other factors, demonstrates that this problem is prevalent enough to warrant consideration in every jury trial. Whether jurors can accurately detect a witness's possible bias or prejudice is another question. See "DETECTING LIES ..." Footnote 73.

[67] I placed the word "improper" in quotes because the law in most jurisdictions provides contradictory guidance to jurors. They are instructed to both consider a witnesses "manner" while he testifies and at the same time consider more objective factors such as the logical coherency of the witness's testimony. "Manner" is simply a synonym for demeanor, and a witness's demeanor includes such factors as physical appearance and conduct.

[68] See Footnote 67.

[69] Boyd, Brian, *On The Origin of Stories: Evolution Cognition, And Fiction*, p. 48 (The Belknap Press of Harvard University Press, Cambridge, MA) (2010). Quoting: Geary, David, p. 170, "The Origin of Mind: Evolution of Brain, Cognition, and General Intelligence, *American Psychological Association* (2005).

[70] "For hundreds of years, judges or juries have decided the credibility of testimony on the demeanor of the witness, including the witness's appearance, attitude, and manner." Hon. Timony, James, "Demeanor Credibility," *49 Cath. U.L. Rev. 903*, pp. 904–905 (2000).

[71] Vaughan, Stephanie, Persuasion Is An Art ... But It Is Also an Invaluable Tool in Advocacy, *61 Baylor L. Rev. 635*, 680–683 (2009).

[72] Hon. Timony, James, Demeanor Credibility, *49 Cath. U.L. Rev. 903*, pp. 904–905 (2000). "[Judges and jurors] often specify the details of their impressions derived from observing the witness testify... findings based on the witness's demeanor ... [reflect] observed behavior, such as *evasiveness, hesitancy, or discomfort while testifying ... twitching, stuttering, sweating, or blinking ...* In the alternative, the [jury] may uphold the witness's [truthfulness] ... *with positive demeanor findings such as honesty and forthrightness, frankness and sincerity, or straightforwardness ...*" (Emphasis added.)

[73] These factors matter not because they are necessarily accurate indicators of a witness's truthfulness but because people think that they are accurate indicators of a witness's truthfulness. The research is mixed concerning jurors' accuracy (or lack of accuracy) when it comes to detecting whether a witness is lying based on the witness's "demeanor." For a good discussion on the various studies that address this issue see, Minzner, Max, "DETECTING LIES USING DEMEANOR, BIAS, AND CONTEXT," *29 Cardozo L. Rev. 2557* (May, 2008).

[74] Everitt, Anthony, *Cicero: The Life and Times of Rome's Greatest Politician*, p. 29, Random House (2003) .

[75] See *Demeanor Credibility* at pp.916–920 (Hon. James Timony writes, "The scope of conduct that encompasses demeanor is quite broad. A witness's demeanor includes the tone of voice in which a witness's statement is made, the hesitation or readiness with which his answers are given, the look of the witness, his carriage, his evidence of surprise, his gestures, his zeal, his bearing, his expression, his yawns, the use of his eyes, his furtive or meaning glances, or his shrugs, the pitch of his voice, his self-possession or embarrassment, his air of candor or seeming levity.")

[76] Hendry, Sarah; Shaffer, David & Peacock, Dina, *Journal of Applied Psychology*, pp. 539–545, (Vol. 74, 1989).

[77] "Liars do not necessarily avoid eye-contact or act nervous." Samantha Mann, Aldert, Vrij & Ray Bull, "Suspects, Lies, and Videotape: An Analysis of Authentic High-Stake Liars," pp. 365–376, *Law and Human Behavior* Vol. 26, No. 3 (June, 2002).

[78] Kelly, Lynn & Keaton, James, "Treating Communication Anxiety: Implications of the Communibiological Paradigm," *Communication Education*, p. 45, Vol.49, No.1 "For the majority of Americans ... public speaking is the most feared communication context." (January, 2000)

[79] See Samantha Mann, Aldert, Vrij & Ray Bull, "Suspects, Lies, and Videotape: An Analysis of Authentic High-Stake Liars," pp. 365–376, *Law and Human Behavior*, Vol. 26, No. 3 (June, 2002).

[80] Hon. Timothy, James, "Demeanor Credibility," 49 *Cath. U. L. Rev.* 903, 904. (Jurors use demeanor to determine truth of witnesses testimony.)

[81] Gardner, Daniel, *The Science of Fear*, p. 6, Penguin Press, New York (2008).

[82] Lynn Kelly and James Keaton, "Treating Communication Anxiety: Implications of the Communibiological Paradigm," *Communication Education*, Vol. 49, No. 1, January, 2000, p. 52

[83] Gardner, Daniel, *The Science of Fear*, p. 65, Penguin Press, New York (2008).

[84] Lynn Kelly and James Keaton, "Treating Communication Anxiety: Implications of the Communibiological Paradigm," p. 52, *Communication Education* (Vol. 49, No. 1, January, 2000).

[85] Pinker, Steven, *How The Mind Works*, "The Smell of Fear," (Excerpted from *The Oxford Book Of Modern Science Writing*, p. 106, Ed. Richard Dawkins, Oxford University Press, (2008).)

[86] Hon. Timothy, James, "Demeanor Credibility," 49 *Cath. U. L. Rev.* 903, 904. (Jurors use demeanor to determine truth of witnesses testimony.)

[87] Lynn Kelly and James Keaton, "Treating Communication Anxiety: Implications of the Communibiological Paradigm," *Communication Education*, Vol. 49, No. 1, January, 2000, p. 52.

[88] Dimitrius, Jo-Ellan, Mazzarella, Mark, *Reading People*, "How to Understand People and Predict Their Behavior—Anytime, Anyplace," p. 18, Random House, NY (1998).

[89] Dimitrius, *Reading People*, 59.

[90] Stephanie A. Vaughan, Persuasion Is An Art ... But It Is Also an Invaluable Tool in Advocacy, *61 Baylor L. Rev. 635*, 680–683 (2009); see also, *Reading People* pp. 57–70.

[91] Vaughan, Stephanie, Persuasion Is An Art ... But It Is Also an Invaluable Tool in Advocacy, *61 Baylor L. Rev. 635*, 680–683 (2009).

[92] Shakespeare, W. (1604, 1994). *Hamlet Act III Scene 2* (A Norton Critical Edition Ed.) (C. Hoy, Ed.). Oxford: W.W. Norton & Company.

[93] Like all of the "stage direction" advice in this book, do this only if it can be done naturally. It depends on where the jury is seated in relation to the person asking the questions, the podium, the attorney's tables and any other possible physical barrier between you and the jury. If you must choose between looking at the jury and

looking at the questioner; look at- and respond to- the questioner. It is always a good idea to visit the courtroom before you testify to familiarize yourself with its physical layout.

94 Pinker, Steven, *the blank slate* (Small case letters in original). *The Modern Denial of Human Nature*, p. 259, Penguin Books (2002).

95 Peterson and Tiedens, Mea Culpa: Predicting Stock Prices From Organizational Attribution, *Personality & Social Psychology Bulletin*, 30:1636–1649 (2004).

96 Gibbon, Edward, p. 325, *The Decline and Fall of the Roman Empire*, Modern Library Paperback Ed. Abridged (1776, 1778, 2003) (Italics in original).

97 Everitt, Anthony, *Cicero: The Life and Times of Rome's Greatest Politician*, p. 29, Random House (2003).

98 Stephanie A. Vaughan, Persuasion Is An Art ... But It Is Also an Invaluable Tool in Advocacy, *61 Baylor L. Rev. 635*, 680–683 (2009); see also, *Reading People* pp. 57–70; Wisotsky, Steven, Sounds and Images of Persuasion: A Primer, *84 Fla. Bar J. 40*, (2010); Dimitrius, Jo-Ellan, Mazzarella, Mark, *Reading People*, How to Understand People and Predict Their Behavior—Anytime, Anyplace, p. 18, Random House, NY (1998); Apple, William; Streeter, Lynn; Krauss, Robert, *Journal of Personality and Social Psychology*, 715–727, Vol. 37 (May 1979).

99 Steven Wisotsky, Sounds and Images of Persuasion: A Primer, 84 Fla. Bar J. 40, 31 (2010).

100 Hon. Timony, James, Demeanor Credibility, *49 Cath. U.L. Rev. 903*, pp. 904–905 (2000).

101 You may also be called as an eye-witness to an omission that constitutes a crime. That is, you may be asked to testify to an action defendant did not perform that he or she is required by law to perform (e.g., Defendant did not feed her infant. Defendant left his toddler in a hot car so that he could gamble in a casino all day etc.).

102 This rule does not apply to expert witnesses.

103 Orwell, G. (1946). *Why I Write* ... p. 105, Penguin Books.

104 Shakespeare, W. (1604, 1994). *Hamlet Act II Scene 2* (A Norton Critical Edition Ed.) (C. Hoy, Ed.). Oxford: W.W. Norton & Company.

105 Winkielman, Piotr et al.,17:799–866, *Psychological Science* (2006).

106 *People of State of Illinois v. Jeryme Morgan*, 25–26, No. 07CR11443, Unpublished Transcript (August 26, 2009).

[107] Orwell, G. (1946). *Why I Write* ... 108–109, Penguin Books.

[108] See, Jensen, V. (2005). "The Science of Persuasion: An Exploration of Advocacy and the Science behind the Art of Persuasion in the Courtroom."*Law & PsychologyReview*. See also,O'Barr & Lind (1981). "Ethnography and Experimentation: Partners in Legal Research" (II ed., Vol. *Perspectives in Law and Psychology*).

[109] *People of State of Illinois v. Jeryme Morgan*, P. 12, No. 07CR11443, Unpublished Transcript, August 26, 2009.

[110] Wisotsky, S., *Sounds and Images of Persuasion: A Primer*, 84 Fla. Bar J. 40, 1,6, 25–26 (2010).

[111] The word "pretentious" is probably a good example of a pretentious word.

[112] Guinier, L., *122 Harv. L. Rev.* 4,73–74 (2008). (Harvard Law School Professor Guinier admired the plain-speaking of Supreme Court Justice Stevens's oral dissent in *Parents Involved in Cmty. Sch. v. Seattle Sch. Dist. No. 1*, 551 U.S. 701(2007), she wrote admiringly about its 'accessibility of style and structure [it was] concise and comprehensible for listeners, [he used] simple language ... plain to the average high-school-educated listener ....")

[113] Quoted by Campbell, James, Lawyering at the Edge: Unpopular Clients, Difficult Cases, Zealous Advocates: Ethical Concerns in Grooming the Criminal Defendant for the Witness Stand, *36 Hofstra L. Rev. 265*, 265 (Winter, 2007).

[114] *People of State of Illinois v. Jeryme Morgan*, Unpublished Transcript No. 07CR11443, 42–43 (August 26, 2009).

[115] *Morgan* at 42.

[116] *Morgan* at 43.

[117] *Morgan* at 3.

[118] *People of the State of Illinois v. Sharon Burton*, 96CR04719, unpublished manuscript (1999) p. 34.

[119] These examples are from actual testimony in completely random bench trials. They are a fairly accurate representation of how some witnesses for the state testify in courtrooms.

[120] Antonin Scalia and Bryan A. Garner, Making Your Case: Art of Persuading Judges, p. xxiii, Thompson/West Publishers (2008).

[121] Samuel H. Pillsbury, *Valuing the Spoken Word: Public Speaking for Lawyers*, 34 Cap. U.L. Rev. 517, 537 (2006). ("*Silence* brief pause provides oral punctuation/ dramatic tension 'This ladies and gentle-

men is the most important point—pause.' Helps with musicality pace and rhythm." *Valuing the Spoken Word* at 537.)

[122] See Adler, Mortimer, *How to Speak How to Listen*, Simon & Schuster (1997). Voice tone should change slightly when emphasizing a point, p. 60.

[123] Elster, Charles, *The Big Book of Beastly Mispronunciations: The Complete Opinionated Guide for the Careful Speaker*, 132 (2nd ed. 2006).

[124] *The Big Book* at 132.

[125] *The Big Book* at 76.

[126] *The Big Book* at 102.

[127] *The Big Book* at 173.

[128] *The Big Book* at 273.

[129] *The Big Book* at 273.

[130] Jansen, Voss, "The Science of Persuasion: An Exploration of Advocacy and the Science Behind the Art of Persuasion in the Courtroom," 29 *L. & Psychol. Rev.* 301, 306 (2005); see also O'Barr & Lind, "Ethnography and Experimentation: Partners in Legal Research," *THE TRIAL PROCESS, VOL. 2 OF PERSPECTIVES IN LAW AND PSYCHOLOGY* 181–207 (B. Sales ed., 1981).

[131] *People of State of Illinois v. Pierre Doty*, No. 07CR05497-04, Unpublished Transcript (2007).

[132] Doty at 17.

[133] U.S. Con. Amend. VI.

[134] *United States v. Havens* 446 U.S. 620, 626 (1980) (Emphasis added.).

[135] *Havens* at 626.

[136] *Havens* at 626.

[137] *Havens* at 626; see also *United States v. Bowens*, 2011 U.S. App. LEXIS 8702 (2011) "'A defendant has the right to have 'a meaningful opportunity to present a complete defense.' Accordingly, 'the right of cross examination is a precious one, essential to a fair trial,' and the defendant should be given 'a reasonable opportunity to conduct cross-examination that might undermine a witness's testimony.'" (internal Citations omitted)

[138] U.S. Con. Amend. VI.

[139] U.S. Con. Amend. VI.

[140] FRE R. 611.

[141] See "Popular Defenses" (this book) for a detailed explanation.

[142] In order for the defense to "preserve" an issue for the appellate court to consider he must have addressed that issue first at trial. There are some exceptions to this rule; however, it is important for you to note that the defense (more than the prosecution) builds his case on two tracts. A good defense attorney considers how his defense will affect the judge or jury; and also, in case of a guilty finding or verdict, how it might assist in defendant's appeal. On the other hand; although the prosecution does have the right to appeal, the prosecution's right is extremely limited when compared to the defense right to appeal.

[143] *Criminal Law Advocacy*, 3-6D Criminal Law Advocacy §6.02D, Matthew Bender & Company (2010).

[144] From the movie *My Cousin Vinny*.

[145] This is a completely made-up word.

[146] Swerling, Jack, "Trial Advocacy: 'I Can't Believe I Asked that Question': A Look at Cross-examination Techniques," 50 S.C. L. Rev. 753, 765 (Spring 1999).

[147] Montaigne, *The Complete Essays of Montaigne*, p. 125. Translated by Donald M. Frame, Stanford University Press (2007).

[148] *Gideon v. Wainwright*, 372 U.S. 335 (1963).

[149] "The thing that hath been, it is that which shall be; and that which is done is that which shall be done: and there is no new thing under the sun." *Ecclesiastes* 1:9 KJV.

[150] The United States Supreme Court held that the standard of proof "beyond a reasonable doubt" applied as the standard of proof in all criminal cases in the case of *In re Winship*. In this case the Court wrote, "The reasonable-doubt standard plays a vital role in the American scheme of criminal procedure. It is a prime instrument for reducing the risk of convictions resting on factual error. The standard provides concrete substance for the presumption of innocence—that bedrock 'axiomatic and elementary' principle whose 'enforcement lies at the foundation of the administration of our criminal law." *In re Winship*, 397 U.S. 358, 363 (1970). (Note: Most courts used "beyond a reasonable doubt" as their standard of proof in all criminal cases before the United States Supreme Court decided *Winship* in 1970.)

[151] See Winship.

[152] The prosecution is not required to prove with 100% certainty that the defendant committed the crime(s) he is accused of committing.

However, perhaps because in many jurisdictions judges are not required to define the standard of proof "beyond a reasonable doubt," the standard of proof is open for manipulation by attorneys when they deliver their closing statement to the jury. For a great discussion of this topic see, Cohen, Jessica, "The Reasonable Doubt Jury Instruction: Giving Meaning to a Critical Concept," *22 Am. J. Crim. L. 677* (1995). In her article Ms. Cohen writes "The U.S. circuit courts and the highest state courts that have directly confronted this issue remain divided in their approaches. The reasonable doubt standard is critical to American jurisprudence. When reasonable doubt is not defined, the jury is left to grope for a meaning. Both the prosecution and the defendant may suffer when the jury applies an incorrect standard of proof. The jury may mistakenly think that the reasonable doubt test requires proof beyond the shadow of a doubt. Likewise, the jury may erroneously interpret the standard as requiring stronger doubts than necessary to acquit." "Reasonable Doubt" at 677.

[153] The following might appear strange coming, as it does, from the author of this book. I think that in many cases this defense ought to work. Investigations regarding the guilt or innocence of a person ought to be conducted with great care and expertise. A defendant should get the benefit of the doubt in cases where the police, prosecutors or other representatives of the state conduct an incompetent investigation. However, the fact that the state (Police, Prosecutors, Lab technicians etc.) made mistakes does not mean that the evidence against the defendant is *therefore* insufficient for a jury to find a defendant guilty. It is 100% certain that some representative of the state has made some sort of mistake in 100% of the criminal cases. The relevant question is not whether someone made a mistake, but rather, the relevant question is whether that mistake (or mistakes) matter. In most cases the mistakes that are made are minor and insignificant. The cases where the mistakes in the investigation rise to the level of calling into question the integrity of important evidence or defendant's guilt are very rare.

[154] *United States v. Crews*, 445 U.S. 463, 470 (1980). "A victim's in-court identification of the accused has three distinct elements. First, the victim is present at trial to testify as to what transpired between her and the offender, and to identify the defendant as the culprit. Second, the victim possesses knowledge of and the ability to reconstruct the prior criminal occurrence and to identify the defendant from her observations of him at the time of the crime. And third, the defendant is also physically present in the courtroom, so that the victim can observe him and compare his appearance to that of the offender."

[155] The courts are suspicious of the accuracy of such pre-trial identification procedures as photo line-ups and show-ups. However, appellate courts do not often reverse the convictions of defendants who claim that they were misidentified by a suggestive identification technique. See, *Neil v. Biggers*, 409 U.S. 188, 196–198 (1972), "We hold that each case must be considered on its own facts, and that convictions based on eyewitness ... identification at trial following a pretrial identification by photograph will be set aside on that ground only if the photographic identification procedure was so impermissibly suggestive as to give rise to a very substantial *likelihood of irreparable misidentification*." (Internal citations omitted and emphasis added.)

[156] I am not even sure what spectral analysis is; however, it sounds like a rhetorical question that a defense attorney would ask in a closing argument.

[157] See Cohen, Jessica, "The Reasonable Doubt Jury Instruction: Giving Meaning to a Critical Concept," *22 Am. J. Crim. L. 677* (1995).

[158] See Cohen, Jessica, "The Reasonable Doubt Jury Instruction: Giving Meaning to a Critical Concept," *22 Am. J. Crim. L. 677* (1995).

[159] In the United States 7th Circuit Court of Appeals discussed the role of evidence *United States v. Lawson*. The *Lawson* case defendant was convicted of selling illegal narcotics. The Appellate court discussed the role of evidence, and what *type* of evidence a jury needs to find defendant guilty. Even though the case is specifically about violation of narcotics laws, the Court's logic is applicable to any case. The Court wrote, "When the defendant is charged with a substantive violation of the narcotics laws, the jury, in order to find the defendant guilty, must be convinced beyond a reasonable doubt that the substance imported was in fact a narcotic drug ... However, it is not necessary that this be proved by direct evidence. 'Just as with any other component of the crime, the existence of and dealing with narcotics may be proved by circumstantial evidence; there need be no sample placed before the jury, nor ... need there be testimony by qualified chemists as long as the evidence furnished ground for inferring that the material in question was narcotics." *United States v. Lawson*, 507 F.2d 433, 438-440 (7th Cir. 1974). (Internal citations omitted and emphasis added).

[160] *Criminal Law Advocacy*, 3-6D Criminal Law Advocacy § 6.02D, Matthew Bender & Company (2010).

[161] See FRE 611 (a)

[162] Clapp, James, *Webster's Legal Dictionary*, p. 279, Random House Reference (1996).

[163] "Convenience store" also known as "Stop & Rob" (in some law enforcement circles).

[164] Antonin Scalia and Bryan A. Garner, *Making Your Case: Art of Persuading Judges*, p. xxiii, Thompson/West Publishers (2008).

[165] *People of State of Illinois v. Turner Reeves*, Unpublished Transcript, p. 12, NO. 02CF 1617 (March, 2005).

[166] An "exacteration" is a word that I made-up. I could not find a real word that expressed this exact idea.

[167] This guideline like all the guidelines in this book, admit of commonsense exceptions. See the "avoid arguing with questioner" section. It is permissible, even advisable, for you to restate the words of the questioner in your answer in order to correct a misunderstanding that might occur by answering the question directly (adding nothing).

[168] Steven Wisotsky, *Sounds and Images of Persuasion: A Primer*, 84 Fla. Bar J. 40, 6 (2010). (*You* control the pace, rhythm, pitch, volume, inflection and pauses. This seems obvious, but it is very important that you control these factors consciously. The best way to do this is to listen to yourself speak and take notice when you are not speaking they way you would naturally speak.)

[169] (Adapted from) *People of the State of Illinois v. Natari Gordon*, p. 38, 0218209, Unpublished Transcript (2008).

[170] ("One common tactic is to instruct the witness to just answer 'yes' or 'no'... I know of no sound authority that permits this restriction to be imposed by counsel. It is also perhaps the most transparent attempt to suppress what the jurors might regard as truthful and desirable testimony. When anticipating this ploy from an opponent, I have always coached my witnesses to respond by reminding the cross-examiner that they have taken an oath to tell the truth and could not agree to just respond 'yes' or 'no' if such answers did not constitute the truth." Melilli, Kenneth, "Trial Technique: Controlling the Non-responsive Witness on Cross-Examination," *32 Am. J. Trial Advoc. 125,135* (Summer, 2008).

INDEX